CW01558091

THE ULTIMATE
SERIAL
KILLER
FACT FILE

by

J. Sutton Parkside

illustrations by

Alison Loomis

ist edition 2023

Please note that this book based on known information about serial killers may be distressing and is intended for informational purposes only.

The actions of serial killers are heinous and abhorrent, and their victims should always be remembered with respect and dignity.

— *J. Sutton Parkside*

"Society wants to believe it can identify evil people, or bad or harmful people, but it's not practical. There are no stereotypes."

— Ted Bundy

Table of Contents

Table of Contents

Introduction

Unmasking Evil

A History of Serial Killers and the Methods Devised to Catch Them

It was a dark and twisted world, one where evil lurked around every corner, waiting to strike. A world where the most heinous of crimes went unpunished, and the innocent lived in fear. But amidst the chaos, there were those who refused to give up the fight. Those who stood up to the killers and brought them to justice. This is the story of serial killers and the methods devised to catch them.

In the late 1800s, a monster roamed the streets of London. Jack the Ripper, as he came to be known, slaughtered at least five women, leaving their mutilated bodies as a gruesome reminder of his savagery. Despite the best efforts of the police, Jack was never caught, his true identity remaining a mystery to this day.

ANOTHER VICTIM OF JACK THE RIPPER.
ALLEGED ATTACK ON PRETTY MISS EISENHART IN THE COOPER HOSPITAL, CAM-
DEN, N. J., SLASHING HER IN A TERRIBLE MANNER.

But the Ripper was just the beginning. In 1904, the French police apprehended Joseph Vacher, a serial killer who had murdered at least 11 people. Using newly developed forensic techniques, including fingerprint analysis and ballistics, they were able to link him to the crimes and secure a conviction.

Across the Atlantic, another killer was wreaking havoc. H.H. Holmes, the "Devil in the White City," had built a hotel in Chicago designed specifically to trap and kill young women. He tortured and murdered his victims before disposing of their bodies in a nearby furnace. But Holmes' reign of terror was short-lived, as he was caught and eventually hanged for his crimes.

As the years went by, law enforcement officials continued to refine their methods. In the 1970s, the FBI developed criminal profiling, which allowed investigators to create detailed psychological profiles of murderers. This technique was used to great effect in the case of the BTK Killer, who terrorized Wichita, Kansas, from 1974 to 1991. After years of frustration, investigators were finally able to use a combination of forensic evidence and criminal profiling to identify and capture the killer.

But perhaps the greatest breakthrough came with the advent of DNA testing. In 1987, DNA evidence was used to convict Tommy Lee Andrews of raping and assaulting a woman in Florida. It was the first time DNA had been used in a criminal trial, and it opened up a whole new world of possibilities for law enforcement officials.

Since then, DNA evidence has been used to solve countless murders, including the case of the Golden State Killer. For decades, this killer had evaded the police in California, leaving behind a trail of fear and death. But in 2018, thanks to advances in DNA testing, he was finally unmasked and brought to justice.

But catching serial killers is not just a matter of technology and technique. It also requires a deep understanding of human behavior and psychology. This was exemplified in the case of Ted Bundy, who killed at least 30 women in the 1970s. Bundy was a master manipulator who was able to charm his way into the trust of his victims. But his downfall came when he was pulled over for a routine traffic stop and the police found evidence linking him to the murders.

Similarly, in the case of Jeffrey Dahmer, who killed at least 17 young men and boys in the 1980s, it was his own arrogance that led to his capture. After one of his victims managed to escape, Dahmer was arrested and eventually sentenced to life in prison.

But even as we celebrate the successes in catching serial killers, we must never forget the victims. Each one was a person with hopes, dreams, and a life that was cut short. It is only by continuing to work towards preventing these crimes from happening in the first place that we can truly honor their memory.

So as we look back on the history of serial killers and the methods used to catch them, we see a story of human ingenuity and perseverance. A story of dedicated law enforcement officials who refused to give up in the face of unspeakable horror. And a story of advances in science and technology that have allowed us to finally bring these monsters to justice.

But we must also acknowledge that there is still much work to be done. Serial killers continue to haunt our streets, and many cases remain unsolved. We must remain vigilant and continue to push the boundaries of what is possible in the fight against these heinous crimes.

As we move forward, we must also remember the lessons of the past. We must continue to refine our methods, using every tool at our disposal to catch these killers before they can strike again. And most importantly, we must never forget the victims, who were taken from us too soon.

In the end, it is only through a collective effort that we can hope to make our world a safer place. It is up to all of us to stand up to the darkness, to fight back against the forces of evil that seek to destroy us. And it is up to all of us to honor the memory of those who have been lost by working towards a brighter, more hopeful future.

SERIAL KILLER FACT FILE:

❖ The FBI estimates that there are between 25 and 50 active serial killers in the United States at any given time.

❖ According to the Serial Killer Information Center, there have been approximately 4,000 serial killers in the United States alone since the 20th century.

❖ It is estimated that serial killers have claimed the lives of over 10,000 people in the United States alone since the 1900s.

❖ Serial killers often have a very high IQ, with an average IQ of 120, compared to the average person's IQ of 100.

❖ According to the FBI's Behavioral Science Unit, serial killers often start their killing sprees in their 20s, and many continue killing well into their 50s or beyond.

❖ The average number of victims per serial killer is estimated to be around 7, but some killers have claimed the lives of over 100 people.

❖ Men are much more likely to be serial killers than women. According to the Serial Killer Information Center, only 17% of all serial killers are female.

* The most common method of killing used by serial killers is strangulation, followed by shooting and stabbing.

* Many serial killers have a history of abuse or trauma in their childhood, and some suffer from mental illnesses such as psychopathy, schizophrenia, or borderline personality disorder.

* The vast majority of serial killers are eventually caught and brought to justice, but some remain at large and continue to kill for years or even decades.Serial killers are individuals who commit a series of murders over a period of time.

* They often have distinct patterns or "modus operandi" in how they select and kill their victims.

* Serial killers may exhibit psychopathic or sociopathic traits, such as a lack of empathy or remorse.

* Many serial killers have a history of childhood trauma or abuse.

* They often have a high degree of narcissism and may seek attention or recognition for their crimes.

* They often engage in behaviors such as stalking, torture, or mutilation of their victims.

* Serial killers can target specific groups of people, such as women, children, or vulnerable individuals.

* They may have a need for power and control, and derive pleasure from inflicting pain on others.

* Serial killers often plan their murders carefully and may carefully select their victims.

* Some serial killers have been known to keep "trophies" or mementos from their victims.

* They may have a history of prior criminal behavior, such as animal cruelty or arson.

* Serial killers can often lead double lives, appearing normal and unsuspecting to those around them.

* Many serial killers have been known to have above-average intelligence.

* They may display a charming and manipulative façade to gain the trust of their victims.

* Serial killers can sometimes have a fascination with weapons or other tools used in their crimes.

* They often have a history of failed relationships and difficulty forming meaningful connections with others.

* Serial killers may have a distorted view of reality and may justify their actions in their own minds.

* They may target strangers or acquaintances, as well as people they know personally.

* Serial killers can often elude law enforcement for extended periods of time, making them difficult to apprehend.

* They may exhibit a lack of empathy or understanding of the consequences of their actions.

* Serial killers may have a history of substance abuse or addiction.

* They sometimes taunt or communicate with law enforcement or the media about their crimes.

* They may engage in rituals or specific behaviors before or after committing a murder.

* They can sometimes have a distorted view of their own actions, minimizing or justifying their crimes.

* Serial killers may have a desire for notoriety or infamy, seeking to leave a lasting impact.

* Serial killers are considered among the most heinous criminals, and their actions are universally condemned by society.

Albert Fish

The Brooklyn Vampire

Albert Fish was born on May 19, 1870, in Washington, D.C., USA, and from a young age, he exhibited odd behaviors and an insatiable appetite for cruelty. As a child, he was fascinated by violence and often mutilated animals.

Growing up, Fish experienced a series of traumatic events, including the death of his father and being sent to an abusive orphanage where he was regularly beaten and subjected to sadistic punishments. These early experiences shaped his dark and twisted psyche, setting him on a path of depravity.

As an adult, Fish's sadistic desires took a horrifying turn. He became a serial killer and a cannibal. He preyed on young children, luring them with his grandfatherly appearance and charming demeanor. Once he had them in his clutches, he would subject them to unspeakable acts of torture, mutilation, and murder.

Fish's crimes were heinous and shocking. He would often write letters to the parents of his victims, detailing the atrocities he had committed in graphic and disturbing detail. He confessed to cannibalism, claiming that he derived pleasure from consuming the flesh of his victims. He became known as the "Gray Man" due to his unassuming appearance and his ability to blend into society, concealing his dark and twisted desires.

Despite his seemingly ordinary facade, Fish's inner demons were unleashed upon innocent children. He was eventually apprehended in 1934 after sending a letter to the family of one of his victims. He was found guilty of multiple counts of murder and was sentenced to death by electric chair.

Albert Fish's chilling biography is a horrifying tale of a man who succumbed to his darkest impulses, inflicting unimaginable suffering on his victims.

FACT FILE:

❖ Albert Fish was known by several nicknames, including the "Gray Man," the "Werewolf of Wysteria," and the "Brooklyn Vampire."

❖ Fish had a history of mental illness, including a diagnosis of religious psychosis, and claimed to hear voices that instructed him to commit heinous acts.

❖ Fish was a sadomasochist and engaged in self-harm, often inserting needles into his own body.

❖ He had a fetish for cannibalism and claimed to have consumed the raw flesh of his victims, including children.

❖ Fish had a long history of sexually assaulting children, both boys and girls, and would often target those who were vulnerable and impoverished.

❖ Fish was married multiple times and had six children, but his family life was marked by dysfunction and abuse.

❖ He had a preference for victims who were African American, as he believed they were less likely to be missed or investigated by the authorities.

* Fish would often write letters to his victims' families, taunting them with details of the horrific acts he had committed.

* He once attempted to castrate himself with a pair of scissors, but failed to do so completely.

* Fish claimed to have had over 100 children as victims, though the actual number is unknown and likely exaggerated.

* He was known to prey on children in his own neighborhood, gaining their trust before luring them away to commit his gruesome acts.

* Fish would often mutilate and torture his victims before killing them, using tools such as knives, saws, and meat cleavers.

* He would sometimes coat his instruments of torture with nails or other sharp objects to inflict more pain.

* Fish once boasted that he "had children in every state," indicating the vast extent of his crimes across the United States.

* He claimed to have had a perverse interest in pain and suffering from a young age, often injuring himself or seeking out pain from others.

❖ Fish had a preference for targeting young boys, and would sometimes dress up in women's clothing to approach them.

❖ He would often send obscene letters to women, describing his fantasies of mutilating and torturing them.

❖ Fish was known to have used aliases and false identities to evade detection by law enforcement.

❖ He would often prey on children at public places, such as parks and playgrounds, where he could easily find vulnerable victims.

❖ Fish had a fascination with cannibalism and reportedly once told a fellow inmate in jail that he would like to bake a child in an oven.

❖ He claimed to have been sexually aroused by pain and suffering, both his own and that of his victims.

❖ Fish was known to have engaged in acts of self-mutilation, including gouging out his own eye and inserting needles into his groin.

❖ He once wrote a detailed account of his plans to abduct, kill, and eat a child, which was later discovered by the police.

* Fish was suspected of having committed crimes in other countries, including Canada, where he had a history of traveling.

* He was considered highly intelligent and articulate, able to manipulate others with his charm and cunning.

* Fish's crimes were considered among the most depraved and shocking of his time, and his trial garnered significant media attention.

* He showed no remorse for his actions and often displayed a disturbing level of enjoyment and satisfaction when recounting his crimes.

* Fish had a history of being in and out of mental institutions, but was often released due to his ability to feign sanity.

* He was ultimately executed by electric chair on January 16, 1936, at the age of 65.

John Wayne Gacy
The Killer Clown

John Wayne Gacy, born on March 17, 1942, in Chicago, Illinois, was a man with a chilling double life. On the surface, he appeared to be a friendly and successful businessman, known for his charity work and involvement in the local community. However, behind closed doors, Gacy harbored dark and sinister secrets.

As a young man, Gacy struggled with his sexuality, hiding his homosexual desires from his conservative family and community. He married twice and had children, but his inner demons eventually led him down a dark path. In the 1970s, Gacy's true nature began to reveal itself.

Unbeknownst to those around him, Gacy lured vulnerable young men and boys to his home with the promise of work or money. Once inside, he would reveal his true sadistic and depraved nature. Gacy brutally tortured, sexually assaulted, and murdered at least 33 known victims, earning him the infamous nickname "The Killer Clown."

Gacy's heinous crimes were compounded by his sickening obsession with dressing up as a clown and performing at children's events, where he would further prey on his victims. He would often bury their bodies in the crawl space beneath his house, creating a nightmarish graveyard right under his neighbors' feet.

Gacy's monstrous actions finally came to light in 1978 when a search of his property uncovered the horrifying truth. He was arrested, and the true extent of his depravity sent shockwaves through the community. During his trial, Gacy showed no remorse, displaying a cold and detached demeanor.

In 1980, Gacy was convicted and sentenced to death for his heinous crimes. His true nature as a sadistic serial killer, masquerading as a respectable member of society, sent shivers down the spines of those who had known him. John Wayne Gacy's legacy remains as a haunting reminder that true evil can lurk behind the facade of a seemingly normal life.

FACT FILE:

* John Wayne Gacy was convicted of murdering 33 young men and boys between 1972 and 1978, making him one of the most prolific serial killers in U.S. history.

* Gacy was known as "The Killer Clown" due to his penchant for dressing up as a clown and performing at children's events while he carried out his heinous crimes.

* He used his position as a contractor and businessman to lure his victims to his home with the promise of employment or money.

* Gacy would often trick his victims by showing them a pair of "trick" handcuffs, claiming to be a policeman, before forcibly restraining them.

* He would sexually assault and torture his victims before murdering them, often using a homemade tourniquet to strangle them to death.

* Gacy kept personal souvenirs of his victims, including their clothing and personal belongings, which he hid in his home.

* He buried 26 of his victims in a crawl space beneath his house, three more in the backyard, and four others in a nearby river.

* Gacy's victims were mostly young men and boys, some as young as 14 years old, who were vulnerable and often from disadvantaged backgrounds.

* Some of Gacy's victims were employees or acquaintances, whom he lured to his home under false pretenses.

* Gacy had a history of violence and sexual assault, including a prior conviction for sexually assaulting a teenage boy, but he was able to evade suspicion and continue his killing spree.

* Gacy's mother, Marion Gacy, was known to have physically and verbally abused him during his childhood, which may have contributed to his violent behavior.

* Gacy was known for his involvement in local politics and charity work, which helped him maintain a façade of respectability in the community.

* He had a disturbed fascination with death and often visited morgues and cemeteries.

* Gacy once confessed to a friend that he would often fantasize about abducting and killing young boys.

* He kept a dog, which he would use to intimidate his victims and prevent them from escaping.

* Gacy had a history of substance abuse, including heavy alcohol consumption and the use of tranquilizers.

* He attempted to rationalize his actions, claiming that his victims "deserved to die" and that he was "helping" them by ending their suffering.

* Gacy sometimes performed sexual acts on his victims' corpses after their death.

* He used various methods to dispose of his victims' bodies, including dumping them in a river, burying them in his crawl space, and disposing of them in a nearby landfill.

* Gacy once buried a victim in his front yard but later dug him up and reburied him in the crawl space when he ran out of space in the yard.

* He used lime to accelerate the decomposition of the bodies in his crawl space.

* Gacy confessed to his crimes in detail during his interrogation by the police, showing no remorse for his actions.

* Gacy's trial was highly publicized and drew national attention due to the shocking nature of his crimes and his alter ego as a clown.

* He pleaded not guilty by reason of insanity, but his defense was rejected, and he was convicted on all counts.

* During his trial, Gacy displayed a disturbing lack of empathy for his victims' families and often made jokes and sarcastic remarks.

* Gacy was sentenced to death by lethal injection for his crimes and spent 14 years on death row appealing his sentence.

* Gacy's final words before his execution on May 10, 1994, were reportedly, "Kiss my ass."

* After his death, Gacy's brain was examined for abnormalities, and it was found that he had a lesion in his brain that may have affected his behavior and impulse control.

Peter Sutcliffe

The Yorkshire Ripper

The Yorkshire Ripper, whose real name is Peter Sutcliffe, was a British serial killer who terrorized the Yorkshire region of England during the late 1970s and early 1980s. Sutcliffe was born on June 2, 1946, in Bingley, West Riding of Yorkshire, and grew up in a working-class family.

Sutcliffe's killing spree began in 1975 and lasted for five years. He primarily targeted women, brutally attacking and mutilating them with hammers, screwdrivers, and knives. His victims were often prostitutes or women he believed to be prostitutes, but not all of his victims fit this profile.

Sutcliffe's killings were characterized by extreme violence and sadistic mutilation, with some of his victims suffering horrific injuries, including severed organs and mutilated bodies. He would often leave his victims in public places, taunting the police and the media with letters and messages.

Despite an extensive police investigation and massive public interest, Sutcliffe managed to evade capture for years, leading to widespread fear and panic in the community. The police pursued several wrong leads and suspects, and Sutcliffe was able to continue his killing spree.

In 1981, Sutcliffe was finally arrested by chance when he was caught with a prostitute in his car. He initially confessed to being the Yorkshire Ripper, but later retracted his confession, claiming that he had been instructed to kill by voices from God. He was eventually convicted of 13 counts of murder and 7 counts of attempted murder in 1981 and was sentenced to life imprisonment.

Sutcliffe's horrific crimes shocked the world, and he became one of the most infamous serial killers in British history. His gruesome acts of violence against innocent women and his taunting of the police and media during his reign of terror left a deep and lasting impact on the community and the country as a whole. Sutcliffe died from COVID-19 in prison on November 13, 2020, at the age of 74, but his chilling legacy as the Yorkshire Ripper continues to haunt the memory of his victims and the public to this day.

FACT FILE:

* Peter Sutcliffe was born on June 2, 1946, in Bingley, West Riding of Yorkshire, England.

* He grew up in a working-class family and had four siblings.

* Sutcliffe left school at the age of 15 and worked in various jobs, including as a gravedigger and a truck driver.

* He was married to Sonia Szurma from 1974 until his arrest in 1981.

* Sutcliffe was known to have a troubled childhood and a strained relationship with his strict father.

* He had a history of violence towards women, including assaults on prostitutes, even before he started his killing spree.

* Sutcliffe began his murderous activities in 1975 and continued until his arrest in 1981, targeting women in the Yorkshire region of England, particularly in the cities of Leeds and Bradford.

* He primarily targeted sex workers or women he believed to be sex workers, but not all of his victims fit this profile.

- Sutcliffe used a variety of weapons in his attacks, including hammers, screwdrivers, and knives.

- His attacks were characterized by extreme violence, with some victims suffering severe head injuries, mutilated bodies, and other horrific wounds.

- Sutcliffe's attacks were often carried out from behind, with him striking his victims repeatedly in the head before mutilating their bodies.

- He would often leave his victims in public places, taunting the police and the media with letters and messages boasting about his crimes.

- Sutcliffe eluded capture for years, despite an extensive police investigation and massive public interest in the case.

- He sent taunting letters to the police, referring to himself as the "Yorkshire Ripper" and mocking their efforts to catch him.

- Sutcliffe's reign of terror caused widespread fear and panic in the community, with women feeling vulnerable and unsafe.

- He used fake license plates on his car to avoid detection by the police.

- Sutcliffe's killings created a climate of fear and suspicion towards sex workers, leading to increased surveillance and stigma against them.

* He was finally caught by chance in January 1981 when he was stopped by the police with a prostitute in his car and found to be in possession of suspicious objects.

* Sutcliffe initially confessed to being the Yorkshire Ripper but later retracted his confession, claiming that he had been instructed to kill by voices from God.

* He was diagnosed with paranoid schizophrenia, but this did not absolve him of his responsibility for his crimes.

* Sutcliffe's trial was highly publicized, and he was convicted of 13 counts of murder and 7 counts of attempted murder in 1981.

* He was sentenced to life imprisonment, with a recommendation that he serve a minimum of 30 years.

* Sutcliffe was initially held in Broadmoor Hospital, a high-security psychiatric hospital, before being transferred to a regular prison in 2016.

* He made several unsuccessful attempts to appeal his sentence and secure his release, causing further anguish to the victims' families.

* Sutcliffe showed no remorse for his crimes, and his lack of empathy for his victims

added to the horror and outrage surrounding his case.

* He was attacked by another inmate with a makeshift weapon in 1996, resulting in injuries to his face and neck.

* Sutcliffe's case led to changes in policing methods, public safety measures, and attitudes towards sex work in the UK.

* He was known for his distinctive appearance, including a gap between his front teeth.

* Sutcliffe's mental health deteriorated over the years, and he was diagnosed with various medical conditions, including diabetes and heart disease.

* Peter Sutcliffe died in prison on November 13, 2020 from COVID-19.

Ed Gein

The Butcher of Plainfield

Ed Gein, also known as "The Butcher of Plainfield," was born on August 27, 1906, in La Crosse County, Wisconsin, USA. He grew up in a rural area with his abusive and controlling mother, Augusta, who instilled in him a warped sense of morality and a belief that women were evil.

As he grew older, Gein's mental health deteriorated, and he became increasingly isolated from society. In 1944, his mother passed away, leaving him devastated and alone. Gein's descent into madness took a horrific turn as he began to indulge in his twisted fantasies.

Between 1954 and 1957, Gein embarked on a macabre spree of murder and grave robbing. He targeted women who resembled his mother, and he would often dig up the graves of recently deceased women and take their corpses home to satisfy his perverse desires.

Inside his farmhouse, authorities discovered a nightmarish scene. Human remains were found throughout the house, including a collection of preserved body parts, gruesome artifacts made from human skin and bones, and furniture crafted from human remains.

Gein's depraved actions shocked the nation and earned him notoriety as one of the most infamous serial killers in history. He was arrested in 1957 and found to be legally insane. He spent the rest of his life in mental institutions, where he was deemed unfit for trial.

Gein's twisted story has inspired countless books, movies, and documentaries, and his horrific acts continue to fascinate and horrify people to this day. Ed Gein's legacy is a chilling reminder of the depths of human depravity and the darkness that can lurk within the human mind.

FACT FILE:

❖ Ed Gein was born on August 27, 1906, in La Crosse County, Wisconsin, and was raised in a small, isolated farmhouse by his controlling and abusive mother, Augusta.

❖ Gein's mother, Augusta, instilled in him a twisted belief that women were evil and fostered a sense of isolation from society.

❖ Gein's mother passed away in 1944, and he became increasingly detached from reality and immersed in his own disturbing fantasies.

❖ Gein's crimes were discovered in 1957 when authorities searched his farmhouse and found a horrific collection of human remains, including preserved body parts and furniture made from human bones.

❖ Among the items found in Gein's house were masks made from the skin of human faces, reminiscent of the character Norman Bates in Alfred Hitchcock's iconic film "Psycho."

❖ The character of Buffalo Bill in Thomas Harris' novel "The Silence of the Lambs" and the subsequent film adaptation was partially inspired by Ed Gein.

- Gein confessed to killing two women, tavern owner Mary Hogan and hardware store owner Bernice Worden, and admitted to robbing graves to obtain human remains for his disturbing collection.

- He would often wear the skin and body parts of his victims, creating grotesque and chilling artifacts from their remains.

- Gein's farmhouse was described as a nightmarish scene, with human remains scattered throughout the property, including a box of noses and a belt made of human nipples.

- He was found to be legally insane and was committed to a mental institution, where he spent the rest of his life.

- Gein's twisted crimes and his fascination with human anatomy and skinning earned him the nickname "The Butcher of Plainfield."

- He was known for his quiet and unassuming demeanor, which masked his depraved and gruesome activities.

- Gein's crimes shocked the small community of Plainfield, Wisconsin, and the nation, leaving a lasting impact on the true crime genre and popular culture.

- Gein's obsession with his mother, Augusta, and his twisted attempts to create a "woman suit" using human skin and body parts reflect his deeply disturbed psychology.

* He was a loner and had very few social interactions, which contributed to his descent into madness.

* Gein's gruesome crimes and bizarre behavior were seen as a reflection of his deeply disturbed upbringing and his mother's influence on his psychological development.

* He was found guilty but not legally responsible for his actions due to his severe mental illness.

* Gein's farmhouse, where he committed his heinous acts, was later destroyed by fire, and the land was eventually sold at auction.

* Gein's story has been the subject of numerous books, articles, documentaries, and movies, perpetuating his chilling legacy.

* He had a collection of human skulls, which he would sometimes use as bowls or decorations.

* Gein had a history of necrophilia and was known to visit graveyards to indulge in his macabre fantasies.

* He would often use his skills as a handyman to gain access to gravesites and steal corpses.

❖ Gein's crimes were seen as particularly heinous due to the gruesome and ritualistic nature of his actions.

❖ He was known to have a morbid fascination with death and would often visit funeral homes and study anatomy books.

❖ Gein's crimes were deemed so horrific that he became a symbol of pure evil in the public imagination.

❖ Despite his horrific crimes, Gein was considered a model prisoner in the mental institution where he was confined, showing no signs of violence or aggression towards staff or other patients.

❖ Gein's infamy and the gruesome nature of his crimes inspired fear and revulsion in the community, leaving a lasting impact on the collective psyche.

❖ Gein's disturbed upbringing, his twisted relationship with his mother, and his macabre collection of human remains continue to be subjects of fascination and speculation in the field of psychology and criminology.

❖ Gein's legacy lives on in popular culture, with his story serving as a dark source of inspiration for books, movies, TV shows, and other media, including the iconic films "Psycho" and "Texas Chainsaw Massacre," which drew upon his disturbing crimes and influenced the horror genre for years to come.

Ted Bundy
The Campus Killer

Ted Bundy was born on November 24, 1946, in Burlington, Vermont. He grew up in a seemingly normal middle-class family, but his charming facade masked a dark and horrifying truth.

Bundy was known for his good looks, intelligence, and charisma, which he used to lure young women into his grasp. He had a dark side that remained hidden from the world for many years.

In the 1970s, Bundy began a gruesome killing spree that spanned several states in the United States. He would often pretend to be injured or ask for help from his victims before brutally attacking and murdering them.

Bundy's crimes were characterized by extreme violence and sadism. He would often sexually assault, mutilate, and kill his victims, leaving behind a trail of carnage and terror.

Despite being a suspect in several cases, Bundy managed to evade capture for years by using his charm and manipulation skills to elude law enforcement. He even acted as his own defense lawyer during his trial, further showcasing his cunning and manipulation.

Bundy's facade finally crumbled in 1978 when he was arrested for driving erratically and found to be in possession of suspicious objects in his car. Subsequent investigations and evidence linked him to numerous murders, leading to his conviction.

During his trial, Bundy displayed a chilling lack of remorse and showed a callous disregard for human life. He was ultimately found guilty of multiple counts of murder and was sentenced to death by electrocution.

Even in the face of overwhelming evidence, Bundy continued to deny his crimes and manipulate those around him. He made multiple escapes from prison, further displaying his cunning and deceitful nature.

Bundy was executed in the electric chair on January 24, 1989, but not before confessing to over 30 murders, though the actual number of his victims may never be known.

Bundy's heinous crimes, his ability to blend in with society, and his manipulation skills continue to horrify and fascinate the public to this day. His story serves as a chilling reminder of the depths of human depravity and the mask of evil that can lurk behind a charming facade.

FACT FILE:

* Ted Bundy was a serial killer who murdered at least 30 young women and girls during the 1970s in several states across the United States.

* Bundy was known for his good looks, intelligence, and charisma, which he used to gain the trust of his victims and lure them into his trap.

* Bundy was a master manipulator, often using fake injuries or posing as an authority figure to approach and abduct his victims.

* He would often sexually assault, mutilate, and kill his victims, sometimes keeping their corpses for extended periods of time and revisiting them.

* Bundy had a disturbing obsession with necrophilia and would often engage in sexual acts with the corpses of his victims.

* He had a modus operandi of bludgeoning or strangling his victims, often leaving them with brutal injuries and mutilations.

* Bundy was known to revisit the crime scenes and the bodies of his victims, relishing in the aftermath of his heinous acts.
* He had a deep-seated hatred for women and would specifically target young, attractive

females, often resembling his ex-
girlfriend.

* Bundy was a skilled escape artist and
managed to escape from jail twice, once by
jumping out of a courthouse window and
another time by crawling through a
ventilation duct.

* During his trial, Bundy represented himself
and showed a manipulative and arrogant
demeanor, attempting to charm the jury and
deny his guilt.

* Bundy used his charm and intelligence to
maintain a facade of normalcy, fooling many
people, including law enforcement, into
thinking he was innocent.

* He had a double life, appearing as a clean-
cut law student and political activist on
the outside, while secretly committing
heinous murders.

* Bundy had a disturbed childhood, with a
troubled family history, and showed early
signs of sadistic behavior, such as
torturing animals.

* He would often revisit the crime scenes and
the gravesites of his victims, engaging in
disturbing acts of necrophilia and
mutilation.

* Bundy had a collection of tools and
weapons, including crowbars, handcuffs, and

a homemade murder kit, which he used in his killings.

* He would sometimes pose as an authority figure, such as a police officer or a firefighter, to gain the trust of his victims.

* Bundy targeted victims in various locations, including college campuses, parks, and residential areas, often stalking them for extended periods of time.

* He would often break into homes, sometimes attacking sleeping victims and inflicting brutal injuries.

* Bundy was known to change his appearance, including dyeing his hair and wearing disguises, to avoid detection by law enforcement.

* He had a complex relationship with his mother, whom he blamed for his actions, and had a history of violence against women in his past.

* Bundy was known to engage in necrophilia, including keeping trophies from his victims, such as body parts and clothing.

* He had a pattern of revisiting the scenes of his crimes and engaging in post-mortem mutilation of the bodies, displaying a sadistic and depraved nature.
* Bundy had a high level of intelligence and was able to manipulate and charm people,

including potential victims, into trusting him.

* He was known to be highly organized and calculated in his crimes, often leaving little evidence behind and changing his tactics to avoid detection.

* Bundy was adept at blending in with his surroundings and appearing normal, making him a master of deception and manipulation.

* He often used deception and manipulation to lure his victims into isolated areas, where he would then attack and kill them.

* Bundy's killings spanned across multiple states, including Washington, Oregon, Utah, Colorado, and Florida, showcasing his ability to travel and evade law enforcement.

* Bundy often engaged in "dry runs," where he would test his tactics and select potential victims before carrying out his murders.

* He had a disturbing fascination with violence and death from an early age, often fantasizing about harming others and indulging in violent pornography.

* Bundy's story has been depicted in numerous books, documentaries, and films, including the movie "Ted Bundy" (2002) and the Netflix series "Conversations with a Killer: The Ted Bundy Tapes" (2019), further cementing his chilling legacy.

David Berkowitz

The Son of Sam

David Berkowitz, known as "Son of Sam," was a serial killer who terrorized New York City during the summer of 1977. Born on June 1, 1953, Berkowitz grew up in the Bronx, New York, and had a troubled childhood. He showed signs of mental illness and had a history of arson and animal cruelty.

Berkowitz's murderous rampage began on July 29, 1976, when he shot and killed Donna Lauria and wounded her friend, Jody Valenti, in the Bronx. Over the course of the next year, he would go on to kill five more people and injure

others using a .44 caliber revolver. Berkowitz targeted young couples sitting in parked cars, often striking at night, earning him the moniker "Son of Sam" in letters he sent to the media and police.

Berkowitz's reign of terror caused widespread panic in New York City, with fear gripping the community as he remained elusive. He taunted the police and the public with cryptic letters and messages, adding to the chilling nature of his crimes. The media frenzy and public speculation intensified as the killings continued.

Finally, on August 10, 1977, Berkowitz was arrested after being caught with a gun in his car. He initially claimed that he was part of a satanic cult and that his neighbor's dog, Sam, had told him to kill. However, he later confessed to all the murders and revealed that he acted alone.

Berkowitz was found guilty of six counts of murder and multiple other charges, and he was sentenced to six consecutive life sentences in prison. He has remained incarcerated since then, showing little remorse for his heinous crimes.

FACT FILE:

* David Berkowitz, also known as the "Son of Sam," killed six people and injured several others during his murder spree in New York City between 1976 and 1977.

* Berkowitz claimed that he received instructions to kill from his neighbor's dog, which he believed was possessed by a demon named Sam.

* He targeted young couples who were sitting in parked cars, shooting them with a .44 caliber revolver, often at close range.

* Berkowitz sent taunting letters to the media and police, signing them with the name "Son of Sam" and leaving cryptic messages that added to the fear and panic in the community.

* He used a variety of disguises and methods to avoid detection, including changing his appearance and using different vehicles.

* Berkowitz often stalked his victims for days or weeks before carrying out his attacks, carefully planning his crimes and evading capture.

* He claimed that he was motivated by a sense of anger and revenge, as he believed that he was commanded to kill by demonic forces.

- Berkowitz had a history of mental illness, including schizophrenia and delusions, which may have contributed to his violent behavior.

- He had a troubled childhood, with a history of behavioral problems, petty crimes, and conflicts with authority figures.

- Berkowitz set over 1,400 fires in New York City before he began his killing spree, earning him the nickname "The Phantom of the Bronx."

- He once worked as a security guard, which allowed him to access restricted areas and gather information about potential victims.

- Berkowitz used different guns in his attacks, and he modified them to increase their firepower and accuracy.

- He carefully selected his victims based on their appearance, often choosing young women with long, dark hair, which he believed resembled his mother, whom he had a strained relationship with.

- Berkowitz would often return to the crime scenes after the murders, watching the police investigation and reveling in the chaos he had caused.

- He once left a note at a crime scene, claiming to be the "Duke of Death" and threatening to kill again.

* Berkowitz used various aliases and fake identities to avoid detection, including posing as a woman and using different names in his letters to the media.

* He had a fascination with guns and knives, collecting a large arsenal of weapons that he used in his crimes.

* Berkowitz kept detailed journals where he documented his thoughts, delusions, and plans for future attacks.

* He would often stalk his victims for days, following them, and learning their routines before making his move.

* Berkowitz's killing spree caused widespread fear and panic in New York City, with people avoiding public places and changing their behavior to protect themselves.

* He was known for his erratic and unpredictable behavior, often displaying a combination of charm and aggression.

* Berkowitz's capture was the result of a parking ticket that led to the discovery of a weapon in his car, which eventually linked him to the murders.

* During his trial, Berkowitz displayed erratic behavior, claiming to be possessed by demons and frequently interrupting proceedings.

❖ He pleaded guilty to the six murders and was sentenced to six consecutive life sentences without the possibility of parole.

❖ Berkowitz has shown little remorse for his crimes, often blaming his actions on demonic possession and refusing to participate in rehabilitation programs.

❖ He has been incarcerated in various maximum-security prisons and psychiatric facilities since his arrest in 1977.

❖ Berkowitz has been the subject of numerous books, documentaries, and films, including the movie "Summer of Sam" (1999) and the docuseries "The Sons of Sam: A Descent into Darkness" (2021).

❖ Despite being in prison, Berkowitz has maintained a small following of admirers and supporters who believe in his claims of demonic possession and conspiracy theories surrounding his case.

❖ Berkowitz has been diagnosed with various mental disorders, including antisocial personality disorder and paranoid schizophrenia.

❖ He has been denied parole multiple times and remains one of the most notorious and chilling serial killers in American history, with his crimes leaving a lasting impact on the communities he terrorized and the field of criminology.

Jeffrey Dahmer
The Milwaukee Cannibal

Jeffrey Dahmer, known as the "Milwaukee Cannibal," was an American serial killer and sex offender who terrorized Milwaukee, Wisconsin, during the 1980s. Dahmer was born on May 21, 1960, in Milwaukee, and his childhood was marked by a troubled family life and early signs of disturbing behavior.

As Dahmer grew older, his dark tendencies emerged, and he began to exhibit an insatiable desire to harm animals and indulge in his gruesome fantasies. In 1978, he committed his first murder, luring a hitchhiker to his home and brutally beating him to death.

Dahmer's killing spree continued for over a decade, with a total of 17 known victims, mostly young men and boys. He would lure them to his apartment, drug them, and then sexually assault, torture, and murder them. He would also engage in necrophilia and dismemberment, often keeping body parts as souvenirs.

Dahmer went to great lengths to avoid detection, employing various methods to dispose of the remains, including dissolving bodies in acid, storing body parts in his freezer, and scattering bones in the woods behind his apartment.

Despite multiple brushes with law enforcement, including an incident where a young victim escaped Dahmer's apartment and alerted police, he managed to evade capture until July 22, 1991, when he was finally arrested after one of his intended victims escaped and flagged down a police car.

During his trial, Dahmer confessed to his heinous crimes, showing little remorse for his actions. He was convicted of 15 counts of murder and sentenced to 15 consecutive life sentences without the possibility of parole.

Dahmer was beaten to death in prison by a fellow inmate in 1994.

FACT FILE:

* Jeffrey Dahmer, also known as the "Milwaukee Cannibal," confessed to a total of 17 murders, making him one of the most prolific serial killers in American history.

* Dahmer's victims were primarily young men and boys, ranging in age from 14 to 33 years old.

* He was known for luring his victims to his apartment with promises of money or alcohol, and then drugging them with sedatives to carry out his horrific acts.

* Dahmer engaged in acts of necrophilia, often performing sexual acts on the bodies of his victims after they were dead.

* He would also dismember the bodies, keeping some body parts as trophies, and disposing of others in various ways, including dissolving them in acid, burying them, or scattering them in the woods.

* Dahmer had a fascination with cannibalism and admitted to consuming the flesh of some of his victims.

* He attempted to create "zombies" by drilling holes into the skulls of some of his victims and injecting them with acid or boiling water in an attempt to keep them alive but under his control.

* Dahmer had a history of mental health issues, including antisocial personality disorder, borderline personality disorder, and psychotic disorder.

* He was known to have a disturbing fascination with dead animals from a young age, often dissecting them and keeping their bones.

* Dahmer was known to have used drugs and alcohol heavily, which he claimed contributed to his violent impulses.

* He was once caught molesting his younger brother, an incident that went largely unnoticed by his family and authorities.

* Dahmer attempted to create a "shrine" with the preserved genitals of his victims in his apartment.

* He kept detailed journals and Polaroid photographs of his victims, documenting his acts in chilling detail.

* Dahmer once convinced a 14-year-old boy to pose for explicit photos, which he used as leverage to keep the boy with him for several days before ultimately killing him.

* He would often perform crude experiments on his victims while they were still alive, such as drilling holes into their skulls and injecting them with chemicals.

* Dahmer was known to have kept human remains in his refrigerator and freezer, alongside his everyday food items.

* He attempted to create a "zombie sex slave" by drilling holes into the head of one of his victims and injecting hydrochloric acid into his brain.

* Dahmer once had a near miss with law enforcement when a young man escaped from his apartment and flagged down police, but Dahmer was able to convince them that the young man was his boyfriend and that they were having a lover's quarrel.

* Dahmer was known for his charm and ability to lure victims with his good looks and friendly demeanor, making him a seemingly normal and unassuming individual to those who knew him.

* He would often engage in acts of mutilation and cannibalism soon after killing his victims, indicating a rapid escalation of his depravity.

* Dahmer was known to have engaged in necrophilia even before he started killing, confessing to having sex with the bodies of dead animals as a teenager.

* He kept a human skull as a decoration in his bedroom and displayed it on a shelf alongside other items.

* Dahmer kept a barrel filled with acid in his bedroom, which he used to dissolve the flesh and organs of his victims.

* He would often return to the bodies of his victims, engaging in sexual acts with them even after they had started to decompose.

* Dahmer would sometimes perform rituals with the bodies of his victims, such as positioning them in suggestive poses or arranging their body parts in a particular way.

* He once attempted to create a "living altar" by nailing the hands of one of his victims to a wooden beam and propping it up in his apartment.

* Dahmer was known to have engaged in cannibalistic acts such as eating the hearts, livers, and biceps of some of his victims.

* He would often keep body parts, such as skulls and genitalia, as mementos in his apartment.

* Dahmer once posed as a police officer to lure a victim into his car, further showcasing his ability to manipulate and deceive.

Belle Gunness
The Black Widow

Belle Gunness, also known as "The Black Widow," was a female serial killer who operated in the late 19th and early 20th centuries in the United States. She was born on November 11, 1859, in Selbu, Norway, and later immigrated to the United States. Belle Gunness is infamous for luring men to her farm in La Porte, Indiana, where she would brutally murder them for their money and assets.

Belle Gunness was known for her charm and beauty, which she used to her advantage to seduce and ensnare wealthy men. She would place personal ads in newspapers seeking romantic companionship and used her allure to attract potential victims to her property.

Once her victims arrived at her farm, Belle Gunness would murder them in cold blood. It is believed that she used a variety of methods, including poisoning, bludgeoning, and dismemberment, to kill her victims. She would then dispose of the bodies on her property, burying them in shallow graves or feeding them to hogs.

One of the most chilling aspects of Belle Gunness' crimes was her calculated and premeditated nature. She would often take out life insurance policies on her victims, forge their signatures, and collect the insurance money after their deaths. She was known to have killed at least 14 people, including her own children, over a span of several years.

Belle Gunness' crimes were discovered in April 1908 when her farm was set on fire, and the remains of several bodies, including those of her children, were found in the wreckage. However, Belle Gunness herself was never found, and it is speculated that she may have faked her death and escaped to avoid capture.

Belle Gunness' ability to charm and deceive, her brutality in taking innocent lives for personal gain, and her calculated methods of murder make her a truly chilling figure in the annals of true crime.

FACT FILE:

* Belle Gunness was believed to have been responsible for the deaths of at least 14 people, including her own children, although the exact number of her victims remains unknown.

* She used personal ads in newspapers to lure wealthy men to her farm, where she would murder them for their money and assets.

* Belle Gunness was born in Norway in 1859 and immigrated to the United States in the late 1800s.

* She settled in La Porte, Indiana, where she purchased a farm that would later become the site of her gruesome crimes.

* Belle Gunness was known for her physical strength, which she used to overpower her victims and carry out her murders.

* She used various methods of murder, including poisoning, bludgeoning, and dismemberment.

* Belle Gunness would often butcher the bodies of her victims and dispose of the remains on her property, burying them in shallow graves or feeding them to hogs.

* She took out life insurance policies on her victims, forging their signatures, and collecting the insurance money after their deaths.

* Belle Gunness was believed to have accumulated a significant amount of wealth from her murders, including money, jewelry, and other valuable possessions.

* She targeted men of Scandinavian descent, as they were less likely to be missed by their families and less likely to be reported as missing to the authorities.

* Belle Gunness was known for her charm and beauty, which she used to gain the trust of her victims and lure them to her farm.

* She manipulated and controlled her victims, isolating them from their families and friends, and gaining complete control over their lives.

* Belle Gunness was abusive to her children, and it is believed that she may have killed them to eliminate them as witnesses to her crimes.

* She hired farmhands who would later mysteriously disappear, leading to suspicions about her involvement in their deaths.

* Belle Gunness had a dark and secretive personality, hiding her crimes behind a facade of normalcy.

* She was known to have had a cold and calculating demeanor, showing no remorse or empathy for her victims.

* Belle Gunness was a loner and kept to herself, avoiding close relationships with others to maintain her secrecy.

* She was skilled at covering up her crimes, cleaning up after her murders and disposing of evidence.

* Belle Gunness was believed to have faked her own death in 1908 when her farm was set on fire, and remains of several bodies, including those of her children, were found in the wreckage.

* She was never officially found, and her fate remains unknown, with some speculating that she may have escaped and lived under a new identity.

* Belle Gunness' case was one of the first instances of a female serial killer in American history, making her crimes particularly chilling and noteworthy.

* Her farm in La Porte, Indiana, became known as the "murder farm" and was notorious for the gruesome discoveries made there.

* Belle Gunness' crimes were the subject of sensationalized media coverage at the time, capturing the attention and horror of the public.

* She had a violent temper, and it is believed that she may have killed out of rage and frustration.

* Belle Gunness' crimes were seen as particularly heinous because she preyed on vulnerable men who were seeking companionship and love.

* She was known to have manipulated and deceived her victims, creating a false sense of trust and intimacy before brutally murdering them.

* Belle Gunness used her farm as a gruesome killing ground, luring her victims there under false pretenses and then brutally ending their lives.

* She was known to have used various aliases and changed her identity multiple times to evade capture and continue her killing spree.

* Belle Gunness carefully planned her murders, choosing her victims based on their wealth, vulnerability, and ease of disposal.

* She left behind a trail of horror, with her victims' remains discovered in shallow graves, dismembered, and mutilated, leaving a chilling legacy of brutality and carnage.

Gary Ridgway
The Green River Killer

Gary Ridgway, born on February 18, 1949, in Salt Lake City, Utah, was a notorious American serial killer known as the Green River Killer. He grew up in a troubled family environment with his parents often arguing and his father being strict and domineering. Ridgway had a low IQ and struggled academically in school, leading to him feeling isolated and rejected by his peers.

As a teenager, Ridgway began exhibiting troubling behavior, including an interest in voyeurism and a fascination with violence towards animals. In 1969, he enlisted in the U.S. Navy and served for 20 years, during which he was stationed in Vietnam and Germany. He married three times and had a son from his second marriage, but his relationships were marred by infidelity and domestic violence.

Ridgway's killing spree began in the 1980s when he started to target vulnerable women, specifically prostitutes and runaways, in the Seattle area. He would often pick them up in his truck, drive to remote locations, and then brutally strangle them. He would sometimes return to the crime scenes to have sexual intercourse with the corpses, and in some cases, he would mutilate the bodies or keep personal items as trophies.

Despite being a suspect early on in the investigation, Ridgway was able to avoid detection for years. He was interviewed by police multiple times and even passed a polygraph test, leading to him being dismissed as a suspect. However, in 2001, advances in forensic technology led to DNA evidence linking him to the murders, and he was finally arrested.

In 2003, Ridgway pleaded guilty to 48 counts of aggravated murder and one count of manslaughter, and he admitted to killing a total of 49 women. As part of a plea deal, he agreed to cooperate with authorities and provide information about his crimes in exchange for avoiding the death penalty. He was sentenced to life in prison without the possibility of parole.

Ridgway's heinous acts and the sheer number of his victims make him one of the most prolific serial killers in American history. He is currently serving his sentence at the Washington State Penitentiary in Walla Walla, Washington, where he remains incarcerated.

FACT FILE:

* Ridgway confessed to killing a total of 71 women, but was officially convicted of 49 murders due to lack of evidence in other cases.

* Ridgway targeted vulnerable women, specifically prostitutes and runaways, in the Seattle area during the 1980s and 1990s.

* He would often pick up his victims in his truck, offering them rides and gaining their trust before brutally strangling them.

* Ridgway frequently returned to the crime scenes to have sexual intercourse with the corpses, and sometimes mutilated the bodies.

* He kept personal items from his victims, such as jewelry and clothing, as trophies.

* Ridgway's killing spree lasted for over two decades, from at least 1982 to 2001, before he was finally caught.

* He was married three times and had a son, but his relationships were troubled and marred by domestic violence and infidelity.

* Ridgway enlisted in the U.S. Navy in 1969 and served for 20 years, including a tour of duty in Vietnam.

* He was known to have a low IQ and struggled academically in school, leading to him feeling isolated and rejected by his peers.

* Ridgway exhibited early signs of violence, including voyeurism and cruelty towards animals.

* He was interviewed by police multiple times during the investigation but managed to evade detection due to passing a polygraph test and lack of evidence.

* Ridgway's case brought attention to the issue of violence against sex workers and the challenges in investigating crimes involving marginalized victims.

* He was known to dispose of the bodies in remote areas, such as wooded areas or along riverbanks, earning him the nickname "Green River Killer."

* Ridgway initially denied any involvement in the murders when first confronted by police in 2001.

* He pleaded guilty to the charges against him in 2003 as part of a plea deal to avoid the death penalty.

* Ridgway showed no remorse for his crimes and was described as cold and emotionless during his court proceedings.

* He was sentenced to life in prison without the possibility of parole, and he remains incarcerated at the Washington State Penitentiary.

* Ridgway was known to lead a double life, appearing as a normal and unassuming person to those who knew him.

* He often targeted victims who were involved in sex work due to the perception that they were less likely to be missed or investigated.

* Ridgway's killings were often premeditated, and he would stalk and plan his attacks on his victims.

* He used various methods to lure his victims into his vehicle, such as offering them money or drugs.

* Ridgway was known to pick up prostitutes along Pacific Highway South, which became known as the "Strip," where many of his victims were last seen alive.

* He used ligatures, such as ropes or cords, to strangle his victims, often leaving ligature marks on their necks.

* Ridgway's victims ranged in age from 15 to 31 years old, with most of them being in their late teens or early twenties.

* He targeted women of different races, including Caucasian, African American, and Asian American.

* Ridgway often returned to the dump sites where he had left the bodies to have sexual fantasies or relive the murders.

* He sometimes moved the bodies to different locations to avoid detection and confuse the investigation.

* Ridgway was known to taunt law enforcement and the media, sending letters and making phone calls to boast about his crimes, further terrorizing the community.

* Despite the overwhelming evidence against him, Ridgway showed no remorse or empathy for his victims or their families, leaving a legacy of fear and devastation in the wake of his heinous crimes.

Aileen Wuornos
The Damsel of Death

Aileen Wuornos was born on February 29, 1956, in Rochester, Michigan, USA. She grew up in a troubled household, and her father was reportedly a convicted child molester who later committed suicide in prison. Wuornos had a tumultuous childhood and began engaging in criminal activities at a young age. She dropped out of school and worked as a sex worker and hitchhiked across the United States.

In the late 1980s and early 1990s, Wuornos embarked on a killing spree that shocked the nation. She was convicted of murdering seven men, whom she claimed had attempted to rape or harm her during her work as a sex worker. Wuornos was known to have a volatile personality and struggled with mental health issues, including a diagnosis of antisocial personality disorder. She had a history of violent outbursts and had spent time in jail for various offenses prior to her murder spree.

Wuornos was arrested in 1991 and her trial gained significant media attention. She initially claimed that the killings were in self-defense, but later changed her story, stating that she had killed the men for robbery and financial gain. Wuornos was found guilty of the murders and sentenced to death in Florida, where the crimes had taken place.

During her time in prison, Wuornos garnered attention and support from some activists who believed she was a victim of abuse and exploitation, while others viewed her as a cold-blooded killer. Wuornos' mental health deteriorated, and she was known to exhibit erratic and violent behavior while in custody.

On October 9, 2002, Aileen Wuornos was executed by lethal injection at the Florida State Prison. Her case has been the subject of books, documentaries, and films, sparking debates about mental illness, abuse, and the death penalty. Wuornos remains a controversial figure in criminal history, remembered as one of the most notorious female serial killers in the United States.

FACT FILE:

* Aileen Wuornos was an American serial killer who was convicted of killing seven men in Florida between 1989 and 1990.

* She was born on February 29, 1956, in Rochester, Michigan, and grew up in a troubled household.

* Wuornos claimed that she had a history of sexual abuse and was abandoned by her mother at a young age.

* She began working as a sex worker at a young age and was involved in criminal activities such as theft and assault from an early age.

* Wuornos had a long history of arrests and spent time in and out of jail for various offenses, including DUI, assault, and robbery.

* She was known to have a volatile personality and was described as aggressive and unpredictable by those who knew her.

* Wuornos' modus operandi was to pick up men while working as a sex worker, shoot them multiple times with a .22 caliber pistol, and then rob them.

❖ She targeted middle-aged men who were seeking sex, and most of her victims were shot in their cars.

❖ Wuornos was known to have engaged in sexual acts with her victims before killing them.

❖ Her first known murder occurred in 1989 when she shot and killed a man named Richard Mallory, who was a convicted rapist.

❖ Wuornos' killing spree lasted for about a year, during which she murdered six more men in a similar manner.

❖ She was eventually arrested on January 9, 1991, after being found in possession of a stolen car and a .22 caliber pistol that was linked to the murders.

❖ Wuornos initially claimed that the killings were in self-defense as the men had attempted to sexually assault her, but later recanted her statement.

❖ She was charged with multiple counts of murder and robbery and was ultimately convicted of seven counts of first-degree murder.

❖ Wuornos was sentenced to death for six of the murders and life in prison without parole for the seventh murder.

* During her trial, Wuornos exhibited erratic behavior and made disturbing statements, including claiming that she enjoyed killing her victims.

* She was diagnosed with borderline personality disorder and antisocial personality disorder, and her mental state was a topic of debate during her trial.

* Wuornos' case gained national attention and was widely covered by the media, making her a notorious figure in the true crime genre.

* She became the subject of several books, documentaries, and movies, including the film "Monster" (2003) starring Charlize Theron as Wuornos.

* Wuornos' case raised questions about the relationship between childhood trauma, mental illness, and criminal behavior, and the role of nature vs. nurture in shaping a serial killer.

* She was known for her angry and confrontational demeanor during her court appearances, often interrupting proceedings and challenging authority.

* Wuornos' troubled upbringing and early exposure to violence were believed to have played a role in her development as a serial killer.

* She was known to have a history of substance abuse, including alcohol and drugs, which may have influenced her behavior.

* Wuornos was executed by lethal injection on October 9, 2002, at the Florida State Prison, becoming one of the few women in the United States to be executed for serial killings.

* She declined to request clemency or appeal her sentence, expressing her desire to be executed.

* Wuornos' final words before her execution were, "I'd just like to say I'm sailing with the rock, and I'll be back like Independence Day with Jesus."

* She is the first female serial killer in the United States to receive the death penalty and be executed since the reinstatement of capital punishment in the 1970s.

* Wuornos' case brought attention to the dangers and violence that sex workers face, highlighting the vulnerability of individuals in the industry.

* Wuornos' story serves as a chilling reminder of the dark and disturbing depths of human behavior, and the devastating consequences of unchecked violence and trauma in an individual's life.

Edmund Kemper
The Co-Ed Killer

Edmund Kemper, also known as the "Co-ed Killer," is an American serial killer who gained notoriety for his brutal crimes committed in California during the 1960s and 1970s. Born on December 18, 1948, in Burbank, California, Kemper had a troubled upbringing characterized by abusive relationships with his mother and a tumultuous family dynamic.

Kemper's first known act of violence occurred at the age of 15 when he shot his grandmother, whom he claimed had been emotionally abusive towards him. He was subsequently diagnosed with paranoid schizophrenia and committed to a mental institution. After his release at the age of 21, Kemper went on to commit a series of horrific crimes.

Between 1964 and 1973, Kemper murdered ten people, including his grandparents, his mother, and six young female hitchhikers. He was known for his large stature, standing at 6 feet 9 inches tall and weighing over 300 pounds, which he used to overpower and brutally kill his victims. After committing the murders, Kemper engaged in acts of necrophilia, dismemberment, and cannibalism.

Kemper's crimes shocked the nation, and he earned the moniker of the "Co-ed Killer" due to his targeting of young female college students. He was known for his calculated and premeditated murders, as well as his ability to appear normal and charming in social settings. Kemper was eventually apprehended in 1973 and convicted of eight counts of first-degree murder.

During his trial, Kemper acted as his own attorney and revealed disturbing details about his crimes, describing his motivations and methods in chilling detail. He was found guilty and sentenced to life in prison without the possibility of parole. Kemper remains incarcerated in the California Medical Facility, where he has been deemed a high-risk inmate due to his violent tendencies and history of killing.

Kemper's case has been widely studied by criminologists and psychologists, and his disturbing acts of violence continue to captivate and horrify those interested in the study of serial killers and their motivations. His life and crimes have been the subject of numerous books, documentaries, and TV shows, contributing to his infamous reputation as one of America's most notorious serial killers.

FACT FILE:

* Edmund Kemper had an IQ of 145, which is considered to be in the genius or near-genius range.

* He began showing signs of cruelty towards animals at a young age, including decapitating his sister's dolls and killing the family cat.

* Kemper's parents divorced when he was nine years old, and he was subsequently raised by his abusive mother, whom he harbored deep resentment towards.

* At the age of 15, Kemper killed his paternal grandparents with a rifle, claiming that he wanted to see what it felt like to take a life.

* After being committed to a mental institution for the murder of his grandparents, Kemper was diagnosed with paranoid schizophrenia and underwent treatment for several years.

* Kemper was released from the mental institution at the age of 21, against the recommendations of his doctors.

* His first two victims after his release were young female hitchhikers, whom he picked up, murdered, and dismembered.

* Kemper had a strained relationship with his mother, whom he blamed for many of his psychological issues and eventually killed in 1973.

* He engaged in acts of necrophilia with his victims' bodies, both before and after dismemberment.

* Kemper often kept parts of his victims' bodies as trophies, including their heads and vocal cords.

* He would engage in conversations with the decapitated heads of his victims, even going so far as to throw darts at them as a form of target practice.

* Kemper confessed to cannibalizing the flesh of at least one of his victims.

* He had a history of picking up female hitchhikers, which he saw as easy targets for his violent urges.

* Kemper was known for his large stature, standing at 6 feet 9 inches tall and weighing over 300 pounds, which he used to overpower his victims.

* He had a deep fascination with firearms and often used guns in his murders.

* Kemper was known for his meticulous planning and execution of his crimes, carefully selecting his victims and covering his tracks to avoid detection.

* He once buried a victim's severed head in his mother's backyard and later retrieved it to engage in further acts of desecration.

* Kemper engaged in "trial runs" to test his ability to pick up and control victims before committing his murders.

* He had a morbid sense of humor and would often joke about his crimes during police interrogations.

* Kemper admitted to feeling a sense of satisfaction and power from taking the lives of his victims.

* He considered himself to be a "sociopathic predator" and showed no remorse for his actions.

* Kemper was known for his manipulation and ability to appear charming and likable, which allowed him to gain the trust of his victims.

* He once killed his mother and a friend of hers, then called the police to confess to the murders and waited calmly for their arrival.

* Kemper had a long history of engaging in violent and sadistic fantasies, which he eventually acted upon.

* He collected newspaper clippings and kept extensive records of his crimes, which he later used to relive the murders.

* Kemper expressed interest in becoming a police officer, and he often socialized with law enforcement personnel.

* He was eventually caught when he turned himself in to the police, stating, "I just wanted to see what it felt like to kill Grandma."

* Kemper was charged with eight counts of first-degree murder and was found guilty on all counts.

* During his trial, Kemper revealed gruesome details about his crimes, including how he mutilated and desecrated the bodies of his victims.

* Kemper was found guilty of eight counts of first-degree murder and was sentenced to life imprisonment without the possibility of parole. He is currently serving his sentence at the California Medical Facility.

H. H. Holmes
Builder of the Murder Castle

Herman Webster Mudgett, better known as H.H. Holmes, was an infamous American serial killer who operated during the late 19th century. He was born on May 16, 1861, in Gilmanton, New Hampshire, and grew up in a troubled household with a strict religious upbringing.

Holmes showed early signs of being a skilled manipulator and a pathological liar. He excelled in school, and as he grew older, he pursued a career in medicine. However, Holmes' ambitions were overshadowed by his dark desires and tendencies towards violence.

Holmes is believed to have committed multiple murders, though the exact number remains unknown. He is infamous for constructing a hotel in Chicago during the 1893 World's Columbian Exposition, which came to be known as the "Murder Castle." This three-story building was designed with hidden rooms, secret passageways, and trapdoors, allowing Holmes to carry out his gruesome acts of murder and dispose of the bodies.

Holmes targeted vulnerable individuals, including women, children, and travelers who were visiting the World's Fair. He would lure them into his hotel, where he would subject them to torture, mutilation, and murder. He would then sell their belongings or use their bodies for insurance fraud schemes, making him one of the first known serial killers to financially profit from his crimes.

Holmes' crimes were eventually discovered, and he was caught and arrested in 1894. He was convicted of multiple counts of murder and confessed to 27 murders, although the actual number of his victims is believed to be much higher. He was sentenced to death by hanging and was executed on May 7, 1896, at Moyamensing Prison in Philadelphia.

FACT FILE:

* H.H. Holmes, whose real name was Herman Webster Mudgett, is often considered one of America's first serial killers.

* He confessed to 27 murders, but the actual number of his victims remains unknown and is believed to be much higher.

* Holmes constructed a hotel in Chicago during the 1893 World's Columbian Exposition, known as the "Murder Castle," specifically designed for his heinous acts.

* The Murder Castle had secret rooms, hidden passageways, and trapdoors that Holmes used to trap and kill his victims.

* Holmes targeted vulnerable individuals, including women, children, and travelers who were visiting the World's Fair.

* He often posed as a wealthy businessman or a caring doctor to gain the trust of his victims.

* Holmes had a charming and charismatic demeanor that helped him manipulate his victims and evade suspicion.

* He used various methods to kill his victims, including asphyxiation, poison, and dismemberment.

* Holmes also used gas chambers and vats of acid to dispose of the bodies, making it difficult for authorities to trace his crimes.

* He was known for altering the construction of his hotel, changing rooms and walls to confuse and trap his victims.

* Holmes was skilled at insurance fraud schemes, using the bodies of his victims to make money.

* He moved around frequently, using different aliases and evading capture for a long time.

* Holmes had a troubled childhood, with a strict religious upbringing and a history of animal cruelty.

* He was married multiple times, but his marriages ended in divorce or abandonment.

* Holmes had a history of fraud and scams, including selling fake inventions and conning investors.

* He had a criminal record that included charges of theft, forgery, and even attempted murder.

* Holmes was known to have a fascination with human anatomy and had a background in medicine.

* He mutilated and experimented on the bodies of his victims after their deaths.

* Holmes engaged in necrophilia, a chilling and disturbing aspect of his crimes.

* He had a network of accomplices who helped him carry out his murders and cover up his tracks.

* Holmes was eventually caught and arrested in 1894 after suspicions were raised about his activities at the Murder Castle.

* He confessed to his crimes and provided gruesome details of his murders during his trial.

* Holmes was convicted of multiple counts of murder and sentenced to death by hanging.

* He showed no remorse for his actions and remained arrogant and unrepentant until his execution.

* Holmes' case was widely covered by the media at the time, making him a notorious figure in American history.

* His story has been the subject of numerous books, documentaries, and movies, capturing the public's fascination with his chilling crimes.

* The true motives behind Holmes' crimes remain a subject of speculation, with theories ranging from greed to sadism and psychopathy.

* H.H. Holmes' horrific acts serve as a chilling reminder of the depths of human evil and the capacity for darkness within the human psyche.

Robert Pickton
The Pig Farmer Killer

Robert Pickton was born on October 24, 1949, in Port Coquitlam, British Columbia, Canada. As a child, he grew up on a pig farm that his family owned, which would later become a notorious site of horror.

In his early years, Pickton was known for his quiet and reserved nature. However, he exhibited an early fascination with the slaughter of animals, often helping out on the family farm and displaying a disturbing obsession with pigs. As he grew older, his behavior became more unsettling, and he was known to be socially awkward and reclusive.

In 1996, Pickton was investigated for an assault on a sex worker, but charges were never laid. It was not until 2002 that his sinister activities were exposed. Police obtained a search warrant for his farm in connection with illegal firearms, but what they discovered was far more horrifying.

Upon searching the property, investigators found human remains scattered throughout the farm, along with blood-stained clothing and personal belongings of missing women, many of whom were sex workers from the impoverished Downtown Eastside of Vancouver. The sheer magnitude of the gruesome discoveries sent shockwaves through the community.

Pickton was subsequently charged with the murder of 26 women, though he was suspected of many more. His farm, which had once been a place of mundane agricultural activity, became known as a grisly killing field where he had lured, tortured, and butchered his victims.

During his trial, Pickton displayed a chilling lack of remorse, and details of his heinous acts were revealed in court, sending shivers down the spines of those in attendance. In 2007, he was convicted of six counts of second-degree murder and sentenced to life in prison with no chance of parole for 25 years, making him one of Canada's most notorious serial killers.

FACT FILE:

* Robert Pickton, also known as "The Pig Farmer Killer," was a Canadian serial killer who targeted sex workers and other marginalized women.

* Pickton was born on October 24, 1949, in Port Coquitlam, British Columbia, Canada.

* He grew up on a pig farm that his family owned, where he later committed his heinous crimes.

* Pickton was known to have a disturbing fascination with pigs and was involved in the butchering and processing of pigs on the farm.

* He was known to lure women to his farm, where he would sexually assault, torture, and murder them.

* Pickton is suspected of killing at least 26 women, although the actual number of his victims is believed to be much higher.

* He would often dismember the bodies of his victims and dispose of their remains in various ways, including feeding them to his pigs.

* Pickton would keep personal belongings of his victims as trophies, including jewelry and identification cards.

* He was known to have a history of violence towards women and had been investigated for assaulting sex workers prior to his arrest.

* Pickton was known for his reclusive and socially awkward nature, often avoiding social interactions with others.

* He had a criminal record that included charges for assault, weapons offenses, and attempted murder.

* Pickton was able to evade detection for years due to the vulnerable nature of his victims and the lack of attention given to missing sex workers in the Downtown Eastside of Vancouver.

* He used his position as a local pig farmer to gain access to his victims, offering them money or drugs in exchange for sexual favors.

* Pickton had a disturbing collection of violent pornography and objects related to his crimes, including restraints and weapons.

* He often boasted about his crimes to acquaintances, but was not taken seriously until his arrest.

* Pickton was finally caught in 2002 when police executed a search warrant on his property in connection with illegal

firearms, and discovered human remains on his farm.

* The sheer magnitude of the evidence found on Pickton's farm was chilling, including blood-stained clothing, personal belongings of missing women, and body parts.

* During his trial, it was revealed that Pickton had bragged to an undercover police officer that he had killed 49 women and planned to make it an even 50.

* Pickton showed a disturbing lack of remorse during his trial, often appearing callous and indifferent to the horrific nature of his crimes.

* He was charged with multiple counts of first-degree murder, but was ultimately convicted of six counts of second-degree murder in 2007.

* Pickton was sentenced to life in prison with no possibility of parole for 25 years, the maximum sentence allowed under Canadian law.

* Some of Pickton's surviving victims have expressed anger and frustration over the police's handling of the case, believing that more could have been done to prevent his crimes.

* Pickton's case prompted significant reforms in the way missing persons cases and crimes against sex workers are handled in Canada.

- He remains one of Canada's most notorious serial killers and his crimes have left a lasting impact on the families of his victims and the communities affected.

- Pickton's farm, which was once a place of mundane agricultural activity, has become infamous as a site of horror and brutality.

- The details of Pickton's crimes, including the gruesome acts of violence he perpetrated on his victims, are chilling and continue to haunt those who learned about them.

- Despite being incarcerated, Pickton has shown no remorse or willingness to take responsibility for his actions, further adding to the chilling nature of his crimes.

- It was revealed during the trial that Pickton had kept a torture chamber on his property, complete with tools and restraints, where he carried out unspeakable acts of violence against his victims.

Richard Ramirez
The Night Stalker

Richard Ramirez, also known as the "Night Stalker," was a notorious serial killer who terrorized the streets of Los Angeles, California in the 1980s. Born on February 29, 1960, Ramirez had a troubled childhood marked by abuse and exposure to Satanic rituals, which would later influence his gruesome crimes.

Ramirez's descent into darkness began early, with his sadistic tendencies emerging in his adolescence. He indulged in drug abuse and developed a fascination with violence and death. In 1984, Ramirez embarked on a gruesome murder spree that would shock the nation.

Armed with a sinister charisma and a penchant for brutality, Ramirez committed a series of heinous crimes that included home invasions, sexual assaults, and murders. His victims, ranging in age from 6 to 83, were chosen indiscriminately. Ramirez left a trail of horror, taunting the police and leaving satanic symbols at the crime scenes, instilling fear in the hearts of the community.

His appearance was as chilling as his actions, with his rotting teeth, wild eyes, and pentagram tattoo on his hand adding to his sinister aura. Ramirez evaded capture for months, leaving behind a trail of mutilated bodies and shattered lives.

However, Ramirez's reign of terror came to an end in 1985 when he was captured by vigilant residents who recognized him. He was convicted on multiple counts of murder, sexual assault, and burglary, and was sentenced to death. Ramirez showed no remorse and reveled in his notoriety, even proclaiming his allegiance to Satan during his trial.

Richard Ramirez died of natural causes on June 7, 2013, while on death row in San Quentin State Prison, leaving a legacy of fear and horror. His name remains synonymous with the dark and depraved world of serial killers, a chilling biography of a man who inflicted terror on innocent victims and left an indelible mark on the annals of criminal history.

FACT FILE:

* Richard Ramirez was born on February 29, 1960, in El Paso, Texas, and grew up in a predominantly Mexican-American neighborhood.

* Ramirez was heavily influenced by his cousin, a Vietnam War veteran who boasted about his gruesome war crimes, including beheading his victims.

* He was introduced to Satanic rituals by his cousin, which later became a recurring theme in his crimes.

* Ramirez had an abusive childhood, with his father physically abusing him and his siblings, and he sustained multiple head injuries as a child.

* He was a heavy drug user from an early age, using cocaine, LSD, and other substances.

* Ramirez began committing petty crimes, such as theft and burglary, at a young age.

* He was known for his distinctive appearance, with rotting teeth, long, greasy hair, and a menacing gaze.

* Ramirez had a history of peeping into windows and sexually assaulting women before escalating to murder.

- He had a wide range of victims, including men, women, and children, ranging in age from 6 to 83 years old.

- Ramirez's killing spree began in 1984 and lasted for over a year, during which he terrorized the residents of Los Angeles, California.

- He often entered homes through unlocked doors or windows, and would then brutally attack and murder his victims with knives, guns, or other weapons.

- Ramirez often left behind Satanic symbols and messages at his crime scenes, adding to the horror and mystery surrounding his crimes.

- He had a pattern of sexually assaulting and mutilating his female victims, sometimes taking souvenirs from the crime scenes.

- Ramirez was known for his erratic behavior, often laughing and taunting the police during his interrogations.

- He was called the "Night Stalker" by the media due to his preference for committing crimes in the dark and his nocturnal activities.

- Ramirez was identified and apprehended by a group of angry residents in East Los Angeles after attempting to steal a car in 1985.

* His capture was a result of a dramatic chase and beating by the angry mob before being handed over to the police.

* Ramirez was found guilty on 13 counts of murder, five counts of attempted murder, 11 counts of sexual assault, and 14 counts of burglary.

* He was sentenced to death in 1989 and spent over two decades on death row.

* Ramirez showed no remorse for his crimes and often made disturbing and menacing statements in court.

* He received fan mail and marriage proposals from admirers during his time in prison.

* Ramirez was known for his fascination with serial killers and often studied their crimes while in jail.

* He maintained his Satanic beliefs and continued to draw Satanic symbols on his body and cell walls.

* Ramirez died of natural causes on June 7, 2013, while awaiting execution on death row.

* His death brought a sense of relief and closure to many of his victims' families and the communities he terrorized.

* Ramirez's trial and crimes were the subject of extensive media coverage and sparked widespread fear and paranoia in Los Angeles during the 1980s.

* Ramirez's case also led to increased security measures in homes, with many residents installing alarm systems and securing their doors and windows.

* Ramirez's childhood home, where he committed some of his early crimes, was reportedly haunted and later demolished.

* His disturbing crimes and evil persona have made him a subject of fascination for true crime enthusiasts and criminologists, who study his case to understand the mind of a serial killer.

Randy Kraft
The Scorecard Killer

Randy Kraft is known as one of the most prolific and sadistic serial killers in American history. Born on March 19, 1945, in Long Beach, California, Kraft grew up in a seemingly normal middle-class family. However, beneath the surface, a dark and twisted persona was brewing.

Kraft's killing spree began in the early 1970s and lasted for over a decade. He targeted young men, often hitchhikers or individuals he picked up at bars, and lured them into his car with charm and manipulation. Once in his control, he would subject them to unimaginable torture, mutilation, and murder.

Kraft's preferred method of killing was strangulation, but he also used poison, blunt force, and other means to end his victims' lives. He often took trophies from his victims, keeping grisly mementos such as Polaroid pictures and personal items as sick reminders of his horrific deeds.

His depravity extended beyond murder, as Kraft engaged in acts of necrophilia and sadistic sexual assault on his victims' bodies. He would often dump their remains along highways or in secluded areas, leaving a trail of death and terror across multiple states.

Kraft was known for his intelligence and cunning, which allowed him to evade capture for years. However, his luck ran out in 1983 when he was finally arrested and convicted for the murders of 16 young men. He was later linked to the deaths of at least 67 victims, although the true number of his victims may never be known.

Kraft's trial was chilling, with gruesome details of his sadistic acts revealed to the public. He was ultimately sentenced to death by lethal injection and remains on death row in California, one of the most notorious serial killers in history, with a legacy of heinous acts that continue to send chills down the spine of those who hear his story.

FACT FILE:

❖ Randy Kraft is believed to have murdered at least 67 young men between 1971 and 1983, making him one of the most prolific serial killers in American history.

❖ Kraft's victims were typically young, vulnerable men, often hitchhikers or individuals he picked up at bars, whom he lured into his car with his charm and manipulation.

❖ He was known for using a "kill kit," which he kept in his car and contained items such as drugs, alcohol, ropes, and other tools he used to incapacitate and murder his victims.

❖ Kraft's killing spree spanned multiple states, including California, Oregon, and Michigan, where he traveled extensively for work.

❖ He often drugged his victims with a toxic cocktail of alcohol and drugs, rendering them helpless before subjecting them to brutal torture and murder.

❖ Kraft had a preference for strangulation as his primary method of killing, using his bare hands or ligatures to suffocate his victims.

* He would often pose his victims' bodies in sexually suggestive positions after death, adding a sickening element of depravity to his crimes.

* Kraft engaged in acts of necrophilia, sexually assaulting the bodies of his deceased victims.

* He would often mutilate his victims' bodies, leaving gruesome wounds and injuries as a sick form of torture.

* Kraft kept detailed notes and photographs of his victims, documenting his heinous acts and treating them as trophies.

* He was known to have kept a "scorecard," where he would mark each victim's name and details, displaying a chilling level of callousness and detachment from his actions.

* Kraft's murders were often premeditated and carefully planned, with him selecting victims based on their vulnerability and availability.

* He would sometimes engage in "road trips," where he would drive for hours, searching for victims along highways and secluded areas.

* Kraft was known to have taken pleasure in the suffering and pain he inflicted on his victims, displaying sadistic tendencies.

* He was known to have engaged in risky behavior, such as picking up hitchhikers or approaching strangers, in order to satisfy his murderous urges.

* Kraft was highly intelligent and cunning, which allowed him to evade capture for years, despite being a prime suspect in several murder cases.

* He was arrested in 1983 after being caught with a dead body in his car during a routine traffic stop, leading to the discovery of his horrific crimes.

* Kraft's trial was chilling, with testimonies from survivors and gruesome details of his sadistic acts revealed in court.

* He was convicted of 16 counts of murder and sentenced to death by lethal injection, a punishment he is still awaiting on death row.

* Kraft's motive for his crimes remains unclear, with no discernible pattern or reason behind his heinous acts of violence.

* He displayed a lack of remorse or empathy for his victims, showing a complete disregard for human life.

* Kraft's crimes shocked and horrified the communities where he operated, leaving a lasting impact on the families and friends of his victims.

* He has been described as a "thrill killer," deriving pleasure and excitement from the act of taking another person's life.

* Kraft's level of sadism and brutality towards his victims was extreme, with evidence of extensive torture and mutilation inflicted upon them.

* He often taunted law enforcement and left cryptic messages at crime scenes, adding to the chilling nature of his crimes.

* Kraft had a history of violence and sexual deviance, with reports of him engaging in aggressive behavior towards others even before his killing spree began.

* He was known to have led a double life, appearing to be a normal, respectable member of society.

* Kraft was known to have used aliases and changed his appearance to avoid suspicion, leading a duplicitous and secretive lifestyle.

* He had a fascination with death and reportedly collected morbid memorabilia, including newspaper clippings and photographs of his victims.

* Kraft's crimes left a trail of fear and terror, as he preyed on young men who trusted him, leaving a chilling legacy of violence and destruction.

Mikhail Popkov
The Werewolf

Mikhail Popkov, known as "The Werewolf," was a notorious serial killer who terrorized Siberia in Russia during the 1990s and early 2000s. Born in 1964 in the city of Angarsk, Popkov grew up in a seemingly ordinary middle-class family. However, his dark and twisted desires would eventually unravel, revealing a sinister and chilling side.

As a young man, Popkov joined the police force and rose through the ranks to become a respected officer in his community. Little did anyone suspect that behind his uniform and friendly demeanor, a cold-blooded killer lurked. In 1992, Popkov committed his first murder, a heinous act of brutality that marked the beginning of his reign of terror.

Popkov's modus operandi was gruesome and macabre. He targeted women who he believed were "immoral" or "unfaithful," using his police authority to lure them into his car under the pretense of giving them a ride home. Once alone with his victims, Popkov would brutally assault and murder them, often using weapons such as axes or screwdrivers. He would then disfigure their bodies in a grotesque manner, mutilating them in a sickening display of sadism.

Despite extensive police investigations and community fear, Popkov remained elusive for many years. He continued to kill with impunity, leaving a trail of terror and horror in his wake. His victims numbered in the dozens, with some estimates reaching over 80.

However, in 2012, Popkov's reign of terror came to an end when he was finally apprehended. Shockingly, it was revealed that he had been living a double life, hiding his monstrous deeds from his family and friends. During his trial, Popkov showed no remorse and was convicted of 78 counts of murder. He was sentenced to life in prison without the possibility of parole.

FACT FILE:

❖ Mikhail Popkov, also known as the "Werewolf," was a Russian serial killer who operated between 1992 and 2010 in Siberia.

❖ Popkov was a former police officer and was known for using his position to prey on vulnerable women.

❖ He was convicted of killing 78 women, but he claimed to have killed up to 81 victims.

❖ Popkov would often offer his victims rides home, posing as a Good Samaritan, before brutally attacking and murdering them.

❖ He targeted women who were often intoxicated or prostitutes, believing they would be less likely to be missed.

❖ Popkov had a gruesome modus operandi, as he would rape, mutilate, and sometimes cannibalize the bodies of his victims.

❖ He would use a variety of weapons, including axes, knives, and screwdrivers, to carry out his heinous crimes.

❖ Popkov would often leave the bodies of his victims in secluded areas, such as forests or remote roads, to avoid detection.

❖ He would sometimes return to the crime scenes to have sexual intercourse with the corpses of his victims.

* Popkov was known to have a "rape and kill" fantasy, and he derived pleasure from the sadistic nature of his crimes.

* He was meticulous in covering his tracks, often cleaning the crime scenes and removing any evidence that could link him to the murders.

* Popkov evaded capture for many years, as the police initially failed to connect the series of murders to a single perpetrator.

* He was finally arrested in 2012 after investigators used DNA evidence to link him to the crimes.

* Popkov confessed to his crimes and showed no remorse during his trial, claiming that he was "cleaning up" his city from immoral women.

* He was convicted and sentenced to life in prison without the possibility of parole, as the death penalty had been abolished in Russia.

* Popkov's case shocked and terrified the communities in Siberia, where he operated, and left a lasting impact on the victims' families.

* It was revealed that Popkov had a history of violence and sexual assault prior to becoming a serial killer, but his actions were never adequately addressed by authorities.

* He had a fetish for women's underwear and would often take souvenirs from his victims as trophies.

* Popkov's wife and daughter were initially unaware of his crimes and were devastated when the truth came to light.

* He used his police uniform and car to gain the trust of his victims, making his crimes even more horrifying.

* Popkov's killings were often premeditated, and he would spend time stalking and selecting his victims before attacking them.

* He had a high level of cunning and intelligence, which allowed him to elude capture for so long.

* Popkov was one of the most prolific serial killers in Russia's history, and his case brought attention to the issue of violence against women in the country.

* He was diagnosed with narcissistic personality disorder during his trial, further revealing his lack of empathy or remorse for his actions.

* Popkov's case prompted changes in the way law enforcement in Russia handles serial killers and improved efforts to identify and track down such criminals.

* He carried out his murders with extreme violence, often inflicting brutal injuries to his victims' bodies.

* Popkov's killings were motivated by a twisted sense of power and control, as he took pleasure in exerting dominance over his victims.

* He used different aliases and disguises to evade suspicion, further highlighting his cunning and manipulation skills.

* Popkov's actions have left a lasting impact on the local communities where he operated, causing fear, mistrust, and trauma among the residents, especially women.

* Even after his arrest and conviction, Popkov remains a chilling reminder of the darkness that can lurk within human beings and the devastating consequences of unchecked violence and brutality.

Kenneth Erskine
The Stockwell Strangler

Kenneth Erskine was born on a moonless night in a dilapidated tenement in London's East End. From a young age, his mind was shrouded in darkness, and his behavior was marked by an unsettling intensity. He had a penchant for dissecting insects and small animals, relishing in the grotesque details of their innards. As he grew older, his fascination with death only deepened.

As a teenager, Erskine's dark tendencies took a darker turn. He became withdrawn and began to display disturbing behavior. He was known to wander the streets at night, lurking in shadowy alleys and preying on unsuspecting victims. His eyes glinted with a sinister gleam as he stalked his prey, leaving a trail of fear and terror in his wake.

In his early twenties, Erskine's dark desires escalated into a horrifying spree of violence. He earned the moniker "The Stockwell Strangler" after a string of brutal murders in the Stockwell area of London. His victims, mostly elderly women, were found with their throats slashed, their bodies contorted into grotesque positions.

Erskine's reign of terror sent shockwaves through the city. He eluded capture for months, taunting the police with cryptic messages and leaving behind grisly clues at each crime scene. His notoriety grew, and the fear of the unseen killer lurking in the shadows gripped the city in a suffocating hold.

Eventually, Erskine's twisted desires led to his downfall. He was caught red-handed, covered in blood, standing over the lifeless body of his latest victim. In court, his eyes gleamed with a chilling madness as he showed no remorse for his heinous acts. He was found guilty and sentenced to life in prison, where his dark presence continues to haunt the nightmares of those who come into contact with him.

Even now, in the cold, sterile confines of his prison cell, Erskine's darkness lingers. He is a specter of terror, a figure of pure malevolence. His mind remains a shadowy abyss, his motives an enigma. The legend of Kenneth Erskine, the Stockwell Strangler, lives on as a chilling reminder of the darkest corners of the human psyche, a cautionary tale of how the line between sanity and madness can blur into something truly terrifying.

FACT FILE:

* Kenneth Erskine, also known as the Stockwell Strangler, terrorized London in the 1980s.

* Erskine was born on January 16, 1962, in London, England, and grew up in the notorious East End.

* From a young age, Erskine displayed a disturbing fascination with death and was known to mutilate animals, foreshadowing his future violent tendencies.

* Erskine's first known murder occurred in 1986 when he was just 24 years old. He broke into the home of an elderly woman, Dorothy Wood, and brutally strangled her to death.

* Erskine's preferred victims were elderly women, whom he targeted for their vulnerability and ease of subduing.

* He often posed the bodies of his victims in grotesque and contorted positions, adding a disturbingly artistic aspect to his killings.

* Erskine would sometimes leave cryptic messages at the crime scenes, taunting the police and instilling fear in the community.

* He evaded capture for several months, creating an atmosphere of terror in London, with the media dubbing him the "Stockwell Strangler" due to the location of his murders.

* Erskine's spree of violence included at least seven known murders, although it is suspected that there may have been more victims.

* He had a history of mental illness, including schizophrenia, and had been in and out of psychiatric institutions prior to his killing spree.

* Erskine's attacks were marked by extreme brutality, often involving strangulation, stabbing, and mutilation of his victims' bodies.

* He was known to stalk his victims, watching them from the shadows before pouncing on them with sudden and vicious attacks.

* Erskine's chilling demeanor during his attacks and in court earned him a reputation as a cold, calculating killer with no remorse for his actions.

* He was finally caught in 1987 when he was found standing over the body of his seventh victim, after a failed attempt to strangle her.

* Erskine was found guilty of multiple counts of murder and was sentenced to life imprisonment with a minimum term of 40 years, ensuring that he would likely never be released.

* During his trial, Erskine showed little emotion and remained eerily calm, adding to his chilling persona as a remorseless killer.

* He had a penchant for leaving behind disturbing and cryptic drawings in his cell, further revealing the twisted nature of his mind.

* Erskine's family history was marred by violence, with several relatives also having a criminal record for offenses such as murder and assault.

* He has been described by psychiatric experts as a "sexual sadist," deriving pleasure from inflicting pain and suffering on others.

* Erskine's crimes were fueled by a deep-seated hatred towards women, whom he viewed as objects of his violent fantasies.

* He has been known to display unpredictable and erratic behavior in prison, making him a source of ongoing concern for prison authorities.

* He has been deemed a high-risk prisoner and is closely monitored due to concerns about his potential for further violence.

* Erskine's case has been studied by criminologists and psychologists as a chilling example of the complexities of criminal behavior and the disturbing nature of serial killers.

* He has been compared to infamous serial killers such as Ted Bundy and Peter Sutcliffe for his heinous acts and lack of remorse.

* He has been known to exhibit disturbing behavior in prison, including making chilling threats to other inmates and engaging in acts of self-harm.

* Erskine has been denied parole multiple times due to the extreme danger he poses to society, and his potential for reoffending is a constant source of concern.

* He has shown no genuine remorse for his crimes, and his cold, detached demeanor has left many unsettled and horrified.

Joseph Christopher
The Midtown Slasher

Joseph Christopher, also known as "The Midtown Slasher," was an American serial killer whose chilling actions left a trail of terror in New York and Buffalo during the 1980s.

Born on January 18, 1955, in Buffalo, New York, Christopher's early life was marked by instability and violence. He had a troubled childhood, suffering from abuse and neglect, and was known to exhibit aggressive and antisocial behavior from a young age. He dropped out of school and became involved in drugs, developing a severe addiction to PCP.

Christopher's descent into darkness took a sinister turn when he was diagnosed with paranoid schizophrenia, a severe mental illness that often involves delusions and hallucinations. Despite several hospitalizations and attempts at treatment, his mental health deteriorated, and he became increasingly delusional and paranoid.

In 1980, Christopher's chilling spree of violence began. He randomly targeted innocent victims, often choosing them based on their race or ethnicity, as he harbored deep-seated racial and ethnic prejudices. He would stalk the streets of New York and Buffalo, armed with a gun or a knife, seeking out victims to satisfy his violent urges.

Christopher's attacks were brutal and merciless. He would ambush his victims, often shooting or stabbing them multiple times, leaving behind a gruesome trail of blood and gore. His actions struck fear into the hearts of the communities he terrorized, as no one was safe from his random and senseless violence.

His chilling actions left at least 13 people dead and several others injured before law enforcement was able to track him down. Christopher's calculated and cold demeanor during his attacks earned him the moniker "The Midtown Slasher," as his killings were centered around the Midtown Manhattan area.

In 1981, Christopher was finally caught and arrested. He showed little remorse for his actions and displayed erratic behavior during his trial, further revealing the depths of his mental illness. He was found guilty of multiple counts of murder and attempted murder, and was sentenced to life in prison without the possibility of parole.

FACT FILE:

❖ Joseph Christopher was born on January 18, 1955, in Buffalo, New York, and had a troubled childhood marked by abuse and neglect.

❖ Christopher's mental health began to deteriorate at a young age, and he was diagnosed with paranoid schizophrenia, a severe mental illness that often involves delusions and hallucinations.

❖ He dropped out of school and became involved in drugs, developing a severe addiction to PCP, which further exacerbated his mental health issues.

❖ Christopher's chilling spree of violence began in 1980 when he randomly targeted innocent victims in New York and Buffalo, often choosing them based on their race or ethnicity due to his deep-seated racial and ethnic prejudices.

❖ He would stalk the streets armed with a gun or a knife, and his attacks were brutal and merciless, leaving behind a trail of blood and gore.

❖ Christopher's victims were often ambushed and subjected to multiple gunshot or stab wounds, resulting in gruesome and horrific deaths.

* He showed no remorse for his actions and displayed erratic behavior during his trial, further revealing the depths of his mental illness.

* Christopher's calculated and cold demeanor during his attacks earned him the moniker "The Midtown Slasher," as his killings were centered around the Midtown Manhattan area.

* He was responsible for at least 13 murders and several attempted murders, instilling fear and terror in the communities he targeted.

* Christopher's actions struck fear into the hearts of people in New York and Buffalo, as his attacks were random and senseless, leaving no one feeling safe.

* He often targeted strangers, making his actions even more chilling, as anyone could become a potential victim.

* Christopher's mental illness and violent behavior were intertwined, with his delusions and hallucinations fueling his urge to kill.

* Despite several hospitalizations and attempts at treatment, Christopher's mental health deteriorated, and he became increasingly delusional and paranoid.

* He had a long history of violence and aggression, both prior to and during his killing spree, displaying a propensity for brutality.

* Christopher's acts of violence were often premeditated, as he would plan and stalk his victims before attacking them, displaying a high level of cunning and calculation.

* He had a deep-seated hatred for people of different races and ethnicities, which fueled his choice of victims, making his crimes racially motivated.

* Christopher's actions caused widespread panic and fear in the communities he targeted, leading to increased security measures and heightened awareness among the general public.

* He had a history of confrontations with law enforcement, often resisting arrest and engaging in violent behavior towards police officers.

* Christopher's mental illness and drug addiction further escalated his violent tendencies, resulting in a lethal combination that made him a highly dangerous individual.

* He exhibited a pattern of escalating violence, starting with smaller acts of aggression before progressing to more heinous crimes, reflecting a chilling progression of his psychopathy.

* Christopher's killings were often carried out with a sense of detachment and coldness, showing a lack of empathy or remorse for his victims.

* He had a history of antisocial behavior, including a disregard for social norms and a propensity for violent outbursts, even prior to his killing spree.

* Christopher's attacks were often swift and brutal, leaving little chance for his victims to defend themselves or escape, adding to the chilling nature of his crimes.

* He was known to have exhibited bizarre and erratic behavior, including talking to himself and displaying signs of extreme paranoia, further highlighting the severity of his mental illness.

* Christopher's killing spree lasted for over a year, from 1980 to 1981, during which he continued to elude law enforcement and strike fear into the community.

* He was eventually arrested in 1981 after a failed attempt to kill a police officer, leading to his capture and subsequent incarceration.

* During his trial, Christopher's behavior remained erratic and unpredictable, with outbursts in court and displays of aggression towards his attorneys and the judge.

* Christopher was found guilty of multiple counts of murder and attempted murder, and he was sentenced to life in prison without the possibility of parole, where he remains to this day.

John Christie

The Monster of Rillington Place

John Christie was a British serial killer whose life was marred by a dark and disturbing history of violence and murder. Born in 1899 in Yorkshire, England, Christie experienced a traumatic childhood marked by a volatile relationship with his father, who was known to be physically abusive. Christie's troubled upbringing, combined with his own personality traits, would eventually contribute to his descent into chilling criminal activities.

As an adult, Christie struggled with alcoholism and sexual dysfunction, which led to the breakdown of his marriage and the dissolution of his family. He worked as a clerk and later as a postman, but his violent tendencies and disturbed fantasies were simmering beneath the surface.

Christie's chilling spree of murders began in 1943 when he killed his own wife, Ethel. He went on to commit at least six more murders, primarily targeting women. Many of his victims were his own tenants, whom he lured to his home under false pretenses, promising them assistance or employment.

The modus operandi of Christie was brutal and calculated. He would strangle his victims, often using his bare hands or a makeshift ligature, and then sexually assault their bodies. He would then hide their bodies in various locations within his property, including the walls, the floorboards, and the garden.

One of the most chilling aspects of Christie's crimes was his manipulation and deception. He framed one of his neighbors, Timothy Evans, for the murder of his own wife and child. Evans was wrongfully convicted and executed in 1950, while Christie continued to kill.

Christie's heinous actions continued for nearly a decade before he was finally caught in 1953. During the investigation, the police discovered the remains of several of his victims hidden in his home, including the bodies of his wife and infant daughter.

He was found guilty of multiple counts of murder and was sentenced to death by hanging. He was executed on July 15, 1953, in London's Pentonville Prison.

FACT FILE:

* John Christie was born on April 8, 1899, in Yorkshire, England.

* He had a troubled childhood, with an abusive father who was known to be physically violent.

* Christie's violent tendencies were evident from a young age when he would often harm animals and exhibit disturbing behavior.

* He served in World War I as a member of the British Army but was discharged due to psychiatric issues.

* Christie had a history of alcoholism and sexual dysfunction, which contributed to the breakdown of his marriage and family.

* His first known murder was the killing of his own wife, Ethel, in 1943, whom he strangled in their London home.

* Christie went on to commit at least six more murders, primarily targeting women as his victims.

* He would lure his victims to his home under false pretenses, promising them help or employment.

* Christie's modus operandi was strangulation, often using his bare hands or a makeshift ligature.

* He would sexually assault the bodies of his victims after killing them.

* Christie would hide the bodies in various locations within his property, including the walls, floorboards, and garden.

* He framed one of his neighbors, Timothy Evans, for the murder of his wife and child, leading to Evans' wrongful conviction and execution in 1950.

* Christie's crimes continued for nearly a decade, during which he lived in the same house where he had hidden the bodies of his victims.

* He had a calm and composed demeanor during his trial, showing no remorse or empathy for his actions.

* Christie was found guilty of multiple counts of murder and was sentenced to death by hanging.

* He was executed on July 15, 1953, at Pentonville Prison in London.

* Christie's case led to significant changes in the British legal system, including the abolition of the death penalty in 1965.

* After his execution, Christie's house at 10 Rillington Place, where he had committed the murders, became infamous and was eventually demolished.

* It was revealed that Christie had kept mementos and souvenirs of his victims, including locks of their hair, hidden in his home.

* Christie's crimes were considered especially chilling due to his deceptive and manipulative nature, leading to the wrongful conviction and execution of an innocent man.

* He had a long history of psychiatric issues, including depression, anxiety, and personality disorders, which were believed to have contributed to his violent tendencies.

* Christie was known to have a fascination with death and had a morbid curiosity about human anatomy.

* He had a deep-seated hatred for women, which is believed to have fueled his attacks on female victims.

* Christie's killings were carried out in his own home, where he lived undetected for years while committing multiple murders.

* He was known to have carefully planned and executed his murders, showing a premeditated and calculated approach to his crimes.

* Christie's chilling actions traumatized the communities he lived in, leading to widespread fear and paranoia.

* He had a history of posing as a doctor and using his medical knowledge to gain the trust of his victims.

* Christie's crimes were discovered when a new tenant moved into his former residence and made the grisly discovery of the hidden bodies.

Jerry Brudos
The Shoe Fetish Slayer

Jerry Brudos was born on January 31, 1939, in Webster, South Dakota, the oldest of two siblings. Despite his outwardly unassuming appearance, Brudos exhibited signs of a disturbed mind from a young age. He developed a fixation on women's shoes, finding solace in the tactile sensation and scent of leather, satin, and lace. As he grew older, this innocent fascination with footwear would take a dark and twisted turn.

Brudos' descent into depravity began in his teenage years when he began sneaking into his neighbors' homes to steal their shoes. He would often engage in voyeuristic behavior, watching women from afar and secretly stealing their footwear as a form of deviant gratification. As he continued to satisfy his growing fetish, he started experimenting with more sinister acts.

In 1967, Brudos committed his first known murder. He kidnapped and killed a young woman, fulfilling his disturbing desires while taking pleasure in the power and control he had over his victim. This brutal act unleashed something dark within him, and Brudos' sadistic tendencies soon escalated.

Over the next few years, Brudos continued to indulge in his twisted fantasies, luring women into his clutches and subjecting them to unspeakable horrors. He would kidnap, torture, and sexually assault his victims, reveling in their suffering. He also developed a macabre habit of collecting shoes from his victims as grim trophies, amassing a chilling collection in his home.

Brudos' double life as a sadistic killer and seemingly ordinary family man continued for years, as he evaded law enforcement and managed to keep up a façade of normalcy. However, his monstrous acts were eventually uncovered in 1969 when he was finally apprehended by the police.

During his trial, Brudos showed a chilling lack of remorse, displaying a detached and callous demeanor. He was convicted of multiple counts of murder and sentenced to life in prison without the possibility of parole. Even behind bars, Brudos maintained his fascination with shoes, often engaging in bizarre and disturbing behavior related to his fetish.

Brudos died in prison in 2006, taking his dark secrets to the grave.

FACT FILE:

* Jerry Brudos was born on January 31, 1939, in Webster, South Dakota, and grew up in a seemingly normal household.

* As a child, Brudos had a fascination with women's shoes, which would later develop into a twisted fetish.

* Brudos began stealing women's shoes from his neighbors' homes when he was a teenager, fueling his deviant desires.

* He exhibited voyeuristic behavior, often watching women from afar and secretly stealing their shoes for his own gratification.

* In 1967, Brudos committed his first known murder, brutally ending the life of a young woman in a fit of sadistic rage.

* He kidnapped, tortured, and sexually assaulted several women over the years, leaving a trail of terror in his wake.

* Brudos kept a collection of shoes from his victims as macabre trophies, showcasing his depravity and obsession.

* He often dressed up in women's clothing and shoes, assuming a grotesque alter ego as he carried out his heinous acts.

* Brudos' wife, Darcie, was aware of his disturbing behavior but turned a blind eye, even helping him dispose of evidence.

* He constructed a "hideaway" in the garage of his home, where he would keep his victims and indulge in his sadistic fantasies.

* Brudos had a dark and violent temper, often subjecting his victims to brutal beatings and torture before killing them.

* He used various methods of restraint, including ropes, chains, and homemade devices, to keep his victims under his control.

* Brudos mutilated and dismembered some of his victims' bodies, engaging in acts of necrophilia and exhibiting a complete lack of empathy.

* He was known to engage in acts of cannibalism, consuming parts of his victims' bodies in a macabre display of his depravity.

* Brudos was a skilled manipulator, able to deceive those around him into thinking he was a normal, mild-mannered individual.

* He was a prolific liar, often fabricating elaborate stories to cover up his crimes and evade suspicion.

❖ Brudos had a disturbing fixation on his own mother, often wearing her clothing and shoes as part of his perverse fantasies.

❖ He kept extensive journals documenting his thoughts, desires, and heinous acts, providing a chilling glimpse into his disturbed mind.

❖ Brudos' dark urges and sadistic tendencies escalated over time, with each murder becoming more brutal and violent than the last.

❖ He maintained a sense of entitlement and superiority, viewing his victims as objects to satisfy his twisted desires without remorse.

❖ Brudos was arrested in 1969 after his wife reported him to the authorities, leading to the discovery of his horrific crimes.

❖ During his trial, Brudos showed a complete lack of remorse or empathy for his victims, displaying a chilling and callous demeanor.

❖ He was convicted of multiple counts of murder and sentenced to life in prison without the possibility of parole.

❖ While in prison, Brudos continued to exhibit bizarre and disturbing behavior related to his fetish for women's shoes.

* He died in prison in 2006, taking his secrets to the grave and leaving behind a legacy of terror and horror.

* Brudos' case continues to be studied by forensic psychologists and criminologists as an example of extreme sexual sadism.

* His collection of shoes from his victims, which he kept as twisted trophies, serves as a chilling reminder of his macabre fetish and the extent of his depravity.

* Brudos' disturbing acts of violence against women and his perverse fantasies continue to be a subject of morbid fascination and horror, as his legacy as a serial killer with a fetish for women's shoes lives on in infamy.

Jane Toppan
Jolly Jane

Jane Toppan, also known as "Jolly Jane," was born on August 17, 1854, in Boston, Massachusetts. On the surface, she appeared to be a charming and caring woman, but beneath her facade lay a dark and chilling secret.

From an early age, Toppan showed signs of disturbed behavior. She was abandoned by her father, and her mother suffered from mental illness, leading Toppan to be sent to various foster homes. As a young woman, she pursued a career in nursing, which gave her access to vulnerable patients and an opportunity to indulge in her twisted desires.

Toppan's reign of terror began in the late 19th century when she started using her nursing skills to harm and kill patients.

She would administer lethal doses of drugs, often a combination of morphine and atropine, to inflict pain and suffering on her victims. She would then revel in watching their agony and death, deriving a sick pleasure from their suffering.

Over the years, Toppan's body count grew, and her killing spree extended to multiple states. She moved from hospital to hospital, leaving a trail of death and devastation behind her. She became known for her manipulative and cunning ways, earning the trust of her victims and evading suspicion.

Toppan's motives for her heinous acts remain unclear. Some speculate that she killed out of a sadistic desire for power and control, while others believe she suffered from Munchausen syndrome, a psychiatric disorder where individuals seek attention and sympathy by fabricating illness or harm in others.

In 1901, Toppan's reign of terror came to an end when she was finally caught and arrested. She was found not guilty by reason of insanity and was committed to a mental institution for the rest of her life.

Throughout her life, Toppan displayed a disturbing lack of empathy and remorse for her actions, often expressing delight and satisfaction in her gruesome deeds. Her case remains one of the most chilling examples of female serial killers in history, leaving a legacy of horror and darkness that continues to send shivers down the spine of those who learn of her twisted life and crimes.

FACT FILE:

* Jane Toppan was born Honora Kelley in 1854 in Boston, Massachusetts.

* She was one of ten children and her father abandoned the family when she was very young.

* Her mother, Bridget Kelley, was deemed "mentally unstable" and was eventually committed to a mental institution.

* Jane was placed in the care of various foster families throughout her childhood.

* She changed her name to Jane Toppan when she began working as a nurse.

* Toppan's nursing career began in Cambridge Hospital in 1885.

* She enjoyed the feeling of power that came with caring for sick people and administering medication.

* Toppan's first known murder was in 1895 when she killed her landlord, Israel Dunham, and his wife.

* She was later suspected of poisoning her foster sister's infant daughter, but was never charged with the crime.

* In 1899, she was hired to care for the Davis family of Cataumet, Massachusetts.

* Over the course of three years, Toppan killed several members of the Davis family, including the father, mother, and two daughters.

* She often used a combination of morphine and atropine to kill her victims, causing them to suffer for long periods of time.

* Toppan would often climb into bed with her victims as they were dying and caress their bodies, deriving pleasure from their suffering.

* She admitted to killing at least 31 people, but some believe her true body count could be as high as 100.

* Toppan's preferred method of killing was poisoning, but she also smothered some of her victims with pillows.

* She enjoyed experimenting with different dosages and combinations of drugs to see how they affected her victims.

* Toppan was known for being a skilled liar and manipulator, able to gain the trust of her victims and avoid suspicion.

* She was eventually caught when a close friend of the Davis family became suspicious of the amount of deaths that occurred in their household.

* Toppan was arrested on October 29, 1901.

* During her trial, she showed no remorse for her actions, claiming that she derived great pleasure from killing her victims.

* Her trial was widely covered by the press, and she became known as "Jolly Jane" due to her cheerful demeanor in court.

* She was found not guilty by reason of insanity and was committed to Taunton State Hospital for the Criminally Insane.

* Toppan was diagnosed with dementia praecox, a form of schizophrenia.

* She spent the rest of her life in the mental institution, where she was known for her strange behavior and erratic outbursts.

* Toppan's case remains one of the most chilling examples of female serial killers in history.

* Her motive for killing remains unclear, with some speculating that she suffered from Munchausen syndrome or a form of sexual sadism.

* Her story has been the inspiration for several books and films, including the 2019 television series "The Alienist: Angel of Darkness."

* Toppan's macabre fascination with death and her victims' suffering is a testament to her twisted and disturbed psyche.

* Her legacy continues to send shivers down the spines of those who learn of her chilling life and crimes.

* Toppan died in the Taunton State Hospital on October 29, 1938, 37 years to the day after her arrest.

Herb Baumeister

The I-70 Strangler

Herb Baumeister was born on April 7, 1947, in Indianapolis, Indiana. He grew up in a seemingly normal family, but would later become known as a notorious serial killer. As a young man, Baumeister displayed an early fascination with death and animals, often engaging in cruel and sadistic behavior. He struggled with his sexuality and married a woman named Juliana in 1971, with whom he had three children.

Baumeister owned a successful thrift store chain called "Save-A-Lot" and was known for his eccentric behavior and love of the outdoors. However, behind his outward façade, he harbored dark and twisted desires. Between 1980 and 1996, Baumeister is believed to have killed at least 11 men, luring them to his secluded property in Westfield, Indiana.

Baumeister's modus operandi was chillingly calculated. He would often pick up hitchhikers, offer them a drink laced with sedatives, and then brutally murder them. He would bury their remains on his property or dispose of them in nearby bodies of water.

In 1996, Baumeister's secret life unraveled when human remains were discovered on his property. He was questioned by the police and initially claimed that the remains were from an old family graveyard. However, as more evidence surfaced, including the discovery of clothing and personal belongings of his victims, Baumeister's façade crumbled.

Realizing that he was about to be caught, Baumeister fled to Canada, leaving his family behind. He was later found dead by suicide in a wooded area in Ontario. His chilling crimes and the horrific discoveries on his property shocked the community and left a haunting legacy. Baumeister's case remains one of the most notorious and chilling examples of a serial killer in the history of Indiana, leaving behind unanswered questions about his motives and the full extent of his heinous acts.

FACT FILE:

* Herb Baumeister was known to have a deep-seated fascination with death and often engaged in disturbing behavior involving animals, such as killing and mutilating them.

* Baumeister had a history of engaging in sadistic and cruel behavior, even as a child. He would often torture and kill small animals, exhibiting early signs of psychopathic tendencies.

* He was married to a woman named Juliana, and together they had three children. Despite maintaining a seemingly normal family life, Baumeister harbored dark and twisted desires.

* Baumeister owned a thrift store chain called "Save-A-Lot" in Indiana, which he used as a cover for his chilling activities as a serial killer.

* He is believed to have killed at least 11 men between 1980 and 1996, luring them to his secluded property in Westfield, Indiana.

* Baumeister's preferred victims were young men whom he would pick up as hitchhikers or at gay bars.

* He would often offer his victims a drink laced with sedatives to incapacitate them before brutally murdering them.

* Baumeister's modus operandi was meticulous and calculated, often burying the remains of his victims on his property or disposing of them in nearby bodies of water.

* He would often engage in necrophilia, performing sexual acts on the corpses of his victims after their deaths.

* Baumeister was known to have exhibited erratic and bizarre behavior, including talking to himself and engaging in self-harm.

* He was known to have a violent temper and would often fly into fits of rage, especially when questioned about his actions.

* Baumeister was known to have constructed a soundproof room in his house, where he would take his victims to torture and kill them.

* He had a fascination with mannequins and would often dress them up and arrange them around his property.

* Baumeister had a habit of burying his victims in shallow graves on his property, often leaving body parts exposed.

* He was known to have kept souvenirs from his victims, such as their clothing and personal belongings, as macabre trophies.

* Baumeister was known to have used aliases and fake names to conceal his true identity and evade detection by law enforcement.

* He had a history of mental health issues, including depression and anxiety, but had never sought professional help.

* Baumeister was known to have a strained relationship with his father, who was reported to have been abusive towards him during his childhood.

* He was known to have a fascination with guns and was often seen carrying firearms.

* Baumeister was known to have engaged in cross-dressing and had a collection of women's clothing that he would sometimes wear.

* He was known to have a secluded and isolated property, which he used as his hunting ground for victims.

* Baumeister's crimes went undetected for years, and he was able to continue his chilling activities without suspicion.

* He was known to have been skilled at manipulating others and was able to maintain a facade of normalcy in his public life.

* Baumeister's crimes left a lasting impact on the community and instilled fear in the area where he lived, with people being horrified by the gruesome discoveries on his property.

* He had a habit of taunting law enforcement, leaving cryptic clues and messages behind, further adding to the chilling nature of his crimes.

* Baumeister's case remains one of the most notorious and shocking examples of a serial killer in the history of Indiana, leaving a lasting legacy of fear and horror.

* He was known to have exhibited a lack of remorse or empathy for his victims, showing a cold and callous demeanor throughout the investigation and legal proceedings.

* Baumeister was known to have meticulously planned his crimes, scouting for victims and creating detailed strategies to lure them to his property.

* He was known to have used various methods of killing, including strangulation, shooting, and blunt force trauma, showing a range of brutality in his actions.

* Baumeister's chilling crimes were finally uncovered in 1996 when human remains were discovered on his property, leading to his identification as a serial killer and his eventual suicide before facing justice.

Elizabeth Wettlaufer

The Angel of Death

Elizabeth Wettlaufer was born on June 10, 1967, in Canada. She pursued a career in nursing, working in various long-term care facilities in Ontario. She initially appeared to be a caring and compassionate nurse, but beneath her outward demeanor, a chilling and sinister personality lurked.

Wettlaufer's dark secret began to unravel in 2016 when she confessed to a psychiatrist about a disturbing pattern of murder. She revealed that she had intentionally administered lethal doses of insulin to elderly patients in her care. Between 2007 and 2016, she was responsible for the deaths of at least 8 elderly residents, and she had also attempted to harm others.

The motives behind Wettlaufer's actions remain unclear. Some speculate that she derived a sense of power and control from taking the lives of vulnerable and helpless individuals. Others suggest that she may have been seeking attention or trying to alleviate her own personal struggles.

What is particularly chilling about Wettlaufer's case is the calculated and concealed nature of her crimes. She carefully manipulated medication records to cover her tracks, making it difficult for her actions to be detected. Her role as a nurse allowed her to have easy access to her victims, and she exploited this trust to carry out her heinous acts.

The revelation of Wettlaufer's crimes sent shockwaves through the Canadian healthcare system and left a trail of horror and grief for the families of the victims. Her actions shattered the trust that patients and their families place in healthcare professionals, and her case raised serious questions about the safety and oversight of long-term care facilities.

In 2016, Wettlaufer was charged with multiple counts of first-degree murder and attempted murder. She pleaded guilty to all charges and was sentenced to life in prison with no chance of parole for 25 years. Her chilling biography serves as a haunting reminder that evil can exist in unexpected places, and that even those who are entrusted with the care of others can commit heinous acts of violence. Her actions have left a dark and lasting impact on the families of the victims and the healthcare community as a whole.

FACT FILE:

* Elizabeth Wettlaufer was a Canadian nurse who was responsible for the deaths of at least 8 elderly patients in her care.

* She worked in various long-term care facilities in Ontario, where she carried out her chilling crimes.

* Wettlaufer administered lethal doses of insulin to her victims, intentionally causing their deaths.

* Her crimes spanned over a decade, from 2007 to 2016, before she was caught.

* Wettlaufer's motives for the killings remain unclear, but it is suspected that she may have derived a sense of power or control from taking the lives of vulnerable individuals.

* She carefully manipulated medication records to cover her tracks, making it difficult for her actions to be detected.

* Wettlaufer had easy access to her victims as a nurse, which she exploited to carry out her heinous acts.

* Her actions shattered the trust that patients and their families place in healthcare professionals, causing widespread shock and horror.

* Wettlaufer's crimes raised serious questions about the safety and oversight of long-term care facilities in Canada.

* She pleaded guilty to multiple counts of first-degree murder and attempted murder in 2016.

* Wettlaufer was sentenced to life in prison with no chance of parole for 25 years.

* She was the first registered nurse in Canada to be convicted of being a serial killer.

* Wettlaufer's case brought attention to the issue of medication safety in healthcare settings.

* She had a history of employment issues and was fired from several nursing jobs prior to her crimes.

* Wettlaufer had a troubled personal life, including a history of mental health struggles and substance abuse.

* She kept a journal where she documented her crimes in disturbing detail.

* Wettlaufer's crimes were described as calculated and premeditated, revealing a high level of planning and deception.

* She targeted elderly patients who were vulnerable and unable to defend themselves.

* Wettlaufer showed no remorse for her actions and remained largely emotionless during her court proceedings.

* She used her knowledge of medical procedures and medications to carry out her crimes without raising suspicion.

* Wettlaufer's crimes were discovered after she confessed to a psychiatrist and turned herself into the police.

* Her case was one of the most shocking cases of healthcare serial killings in Canadian history.

* Wettlaufer's actions left a deep and lasting impact on the families of the victims, who had trusted her with their loved ones' care.

* She received significant media attention during her trial, with many people expressing shock and horror at the extent of her crimes.

* Wettlaufer's case resulted in increased scrutiny and regulations for long-term care facilities in Canada, aimed at preventing similar tragedies.

* She is currently serving her sentence in prison and will not be eligible for parole for 25 years.

* Wettlaufer's chilling crimes have forever stained her nursing career and left a dark legacy of betrayal and tragedy.

* Her case serves as a stark reminder that evil can exist in unexpected places, and that even those entrusted with the care of others can commit heinous acts.

* Wettlaufer's lack of remorse and calculated actions during her crimes continue to send chills down the spines of those who hear her story.

* Her case stands as a chilling reminder of the depths of human depravity and the devastating consequences of betrayal and abuse in healthcare settings.

Samuel Little
The Choke and Stroke Killer

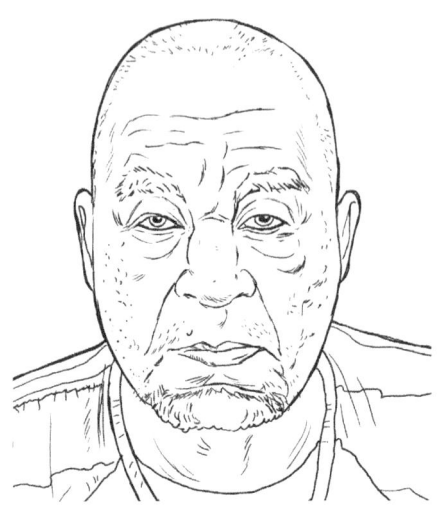

Samuel Little, born on June 7, 1940, was a man with a dark and twisted past that sent chills down the spines of those who crossed his path. Growing up in a small town in the Midwest, Little was known for his quiet and unassuming demeanor, but underneath his unassuming exterior lurked a malevolent darkness.

At a young age, Little displayed a fascination with violence and a penchant for cruelty. He was known to torture small animals and exhibit disturbing behavior that disturbed those around him. As he grew older, his dark tendencies intensified, and he began to show an insatiable appetite for inflicting pain on others.

Little's reign of terror began in the late 1960s when he embarked on a killing spree that spanned across multiple states in the United States. He targeted vulnerable women, often those who were marginalized and overlooked, such as sex workers and those struggling with addiction. He would lure them in with a charming facade, gaining their trust before brutally ending their lives.

What made Little truly chilling was his ability to evade law enforcement for decades. He was skilled at covering his tracks, moving from place to place, and changing his identity. He left a trail of bodies in his wake, but the lack of evidence and his ability to blend in made him a ghost-like figure, haunting communities with fear.

It wasn't until the early 2010s that Little's reign of terror finally came to an end. He was eventually arrested and convicted for multiple counts of murder, revealing the gruesome details of his crimes during his trial. The sheer brutality of his actions and the calculated manner in which he carried out his killings sent shivers down the spines of those in the courtroom.

Even after his capture, Little's chilling biography continued to unravel. He confessed to over 90 murders, making him one of the most prolific serial killers in American history.

FACT FILE:

- Samuel Little was born on June 7, 1940, in Reynolds, Georgia, and grew up in a dysfunctional household with an abusive mother.

- He claimed to have begun his killing spree in 1970 and continued to commit murders for over four decades.

- Little targeted vulnerable women, often targeting sex workers, drug addicts, and those living on the margins of society.

- He was known for his charm and ability to gain the trust of his victims before brutally ending their lives.

- Little traveled extensively across the United States, committing murders in multiple states including California, Florida, Texas, and Ohio.

- He often strangled his victims, leaving minimal evidence and making it difficult for law enforcement to link the deaths to him.

- Little was known to move frequently, changing his name and identity to evade capture.

* He was arrested and convicted multiple times for various crimes, including assault, rape, and theft, but managed to avoid detection as a serial killer for decades.

* Little was known to keep mementos from his victims, such as jewelry or clothing, as twisted souvenirs.

* He had a photographic memory and could recall intricate details about his victims and the murders he committed, which helped him evade capture for years.

* Little confessed to killing over 90 people, making him one of the most prolific serial killers in American history.

* He often targeted women of color, taking advantage of their marginalized status to avoid scrutiny from law enforcement.

* Little was skilled at manipulating his victims and would often use drugs or alcohol to subdue them before committing his heinous acts.

* He had a history of violence towards women, with prior arrests and convictions for attacking and injuring women.

* Little had a history of engaging in extreme violence, including beating, strangling, and mutilating his victims.

* He claimed to have committed murders in at least 19 states, leaving a trail of death and terror across the country.

* Little had a twisted fascination with death and would often visit the gravesites of his victims after their murders.

* He was known to move from city to city, targeting vulnerable women in different locations, making it difficult for law enforcement to connect the murders.

* Little would often pose as a good Samaritan, offering rides or assistance to his victims before betraying their trust and taking their lives.

* He showed no remorse for his actions, often describing the murders in chilling detail during police interrogations.

* Little had a pattern of targeting victims who resembled women from his past, including his mother and former romantic partners.

* He often chose remote or isolated locations to commit his murders, increasing the difficulty of discovering the bodies.

* Little was known to dispose of the bodies in a haphazard manner, making it challenging for law enforcement to recover evidence.

* He had a history of escaping from custody, including once escaping from a detention center in Mississippi and remaining at large for over a month.

* Little's crimes remained undetected for years, allowing him to continue his killing spree without being caught.

* He had a volatile personality, with a history of violent outbursts and a short temper.

* Little was known to taunt law enforcement, often sending letters or drawings to police boasting about his crimes.

* He had a history of substance abuse, including alcohol and drugs, which he often used to manipulate and subdue his victims.

* Little claimed to have committed his first murder at the age of 14, demonstrating a disturbing pattern of violence from a young age.

* He died in prison on December 30, 2020, taking the details of many of his murders to his grave, leaving unanswered questions and a chilling legacy.

John George Haigh
The Acid Bath Murderer

John George Haigh, also known as the "Acid Bath Murderer," was a British serial killer who committed a series of gruesome crimes in the 1940s. Born in 1909 in Lincolnshire, England, Haigh was raised in a middle-class family and displayed early signs of a disturbed mind.

As a teenager, Haigh became interested in the occult and the supernatural. He also began to steal, leading to his first criminal conviction in 1924 for theft. Over the years, Haigh's criminal activities escalated, and he was eventually convicted for fraud and served time in prison.

Haigh's killing spree began in the late 1940s when he turned to a macabre method of murder - dissolving his victims' bodies in sulfuric acid. He believed that this method would destroy all evidence, leaving no trace of his gruesome crimes behind.

Haigh's victims were largely people he knew, including former acquaintances and business partners. He would lure them to his workshop, where he would brutally kill them before dissolving their bodies in barrels of acid. He later claimed that he drank the resulting sludge, believing that it would prevent his crimes from being discovered.

After several murders, Haigh's killing spree came to an end in 1949 when he was finally caught by the authorities. Haigh was arrested for the murder of Dr. Archibald Henderson, a wealthy businessman whom he had lured to his workshop and killed before dissolving his body in acid.

During his trial, Haigh's chilling testimony left the courtroom in shock. He calmly described his crimes and showed no remorse for his actions. He even claimed that he had drunk the blood of his victims in an attempt to gain their power.

Haigh was convicted and sentenced to death by hanging, and his case gained notoriety as one of the most gruesome and bizarre in British criminal history. His macabre method of using acid to dissolve bodies and his lack of remorse for his actions make him a haunting figure in the annals of true crime history.

FACT FILE:

- John George Haigh was born on July 24, 1909, in Lincolnshire, England.

- He had a troubled childhood and was known to be a loner, often engaging in acts of petty theft.

- Haigh claimed to have had an interest in the occult and supernatural, which may have influenced his later actions.

- He had a history of fraud and served time in prison for his criminal activities.

- Haigh's killing spree began in the late 1940s when he turned to dissolving his victims' bodies in sulfuric acid.

- He believed that acid would destroy all evidence of his crimes, leaving no trace behind.

- Haigh's victims were primarily people he knew, including former acquaintances and business partners.

- He would lure his victims to his workshop, where he would brutally kill them before dissolving their bodies in barrels of acid.

- Haigh claimed to have drunk the sludge that resulted from dissolving his victims' bodies, believing it would prevent his crimes from being discovered.

* He showed no remorse for his actions and viewed his victims as mere objects to be disposed of.

* Haigh was known for his calm and composed demeanor, even during his trial for murder.

* He shocked the courtroom with his chilling testimony, calmly describing his crimes in detail.

* Haigh claimed that he drank the blood of his victims in an attempt to gain their power.

* He was known to have meticulously planned his murders to avoid detection, displaying a high level of premeditation.

* Haigh used various aliases and fake identities to evade suspicion and commit his crimes.

* He had a fascination with chemistry and used his knowledge to dissolve bodies in acid.

* Haigh's method of using acid to dispose of bodies earned him the nickname "Acid Bath Murderer."

* He is believed to have murdered at least six people, although he confessed to killing nine.

- Haigh's crimes were discovered when he was arrested for the murder of Dr. Archibald Henderson.

- He claimed that he committed the murders to fund a lavish lifestyle and avoid debts.

- Haigh's trial was highly publicized and captivated the attention of the public and the media.

- He was convicted of murder and sentenced to death by hanging.

- Haigh's case is considered one of the most gruesome and bizarre in British criminal history.

- He is believed to have shown psychopathic traits, including a lack of empathy and remorse.

- Haigh's crimes were seen as heinous and shocking, as the method of using acid to dissolve bodies was highly unusual and brutal.

- He is considered one of the most notorious serial killers in British history.

- Haigh's case led to changes in forensic science and criminal investigation techniques to better detect dissolved bodies.

- He was executed by hanging on August 10, 1949, at Wandsworth Prison in London.

Fred and Rose West

The House of Horrors

Fred and Rose West were a notorious husband-and-wife duo who gained infamy as serial killers in the United Kingdom. They were born in the 1940s and grew up in the Gloucester area of England.

Fred West was known for his violent and abusive behavior from a young age. He had a history of sexual assault and was often in trouble with the law. He married his first wife, Rena, in 1962 and had three children with her. However, Fred's violent tendencies continued, and he became known for his extreme sadism and sexual deviancy.

Rose West, born Rosemary Letts, grew up in a dysfunctional family and faced sexual abuse from her father. She was known to be manipulative and had a history of violence, including assault and theft. She married Fred in 1972 after a turbulent relationship and became an accomplice in his horrific crimes.

The Wests' killing spree began in the 1970s and lasted for over two decades. They preyed on vulnerable young women and girls, often targeting those who were homeless or had a troubled background. The victims were lured to their home at 25 Cromwell Street, where they were subjected to brutal sexual assaults, torture, and murder.

The Wests' crimes were gruesome and horrific. They were known to have tortured their victims using various methods, including strangulation, suffocation, and dismemberment. Some of the victims were buried in the cellar or garden of their home, while others were dismembered and hidden in various locations.

The Wests' crimes went undetected for years, and they continued to live a seemingly normal life, raising their children and maintaining a facade of respectability. However, in 1994, their crimes were uncovered when one of their daughters revealed the extent of the abuse they had endured and the horrors that had taken place in their home.

The subsequent police investigation uncovered a house of horrors, with evidence of multiple murders and acts of depravity. Fred and Rose West were arrested and charged with multiple counts of murder, rape, and torture.

The shocking nature of the Wests' crimes sent shockwaves through the community and gained international attention. They were both convicted of murder and other charges, with Fred ultimately taking his own life by hanging in his jail cell in 1995. Rose was sentenced to life in prison without the possibility of parole.

The case of Fred and Rose West is considered one of the most disturbing and chilling in criminal history. It shed light on the depths of human depravity and the horrors that can occur within seemingly normal households. Their legacy as brutal serial killers continues to haunt and shock the public to this day.

FACT FILE:

❖ Fred and Rose West were convicted of murdering at least 12 young women and girls between the 1960s and 1980s, making them one of Britain's most notorious serial killer couples.

❖ Fred West was known for his violent and abusive behavior from a young age, and he had a history of sexual assault and criminal activities.

❖ Rose West had a troubled childhood, with a history of sexual abuse by her father and a reputation for being manipulative and violent.

❖ The Wests' victims were often young women and girls who were vulnerable and easily exploited, including runaways, hitchhikers, and girls from troubled backgrounds.

❖ The Wests' crimes were characterized by extreme sadism, torture, and sexual deviancy, with evidence of horrific acts of violence inflicted upon their victims.

❖ The Wests would often lure their victims to their home at 25 Cromwell Street in Gloucester, England, under false pretenses before subjecting them to brutal assaults.

* The victims were often strangled or suffocated to death, and their bodies were then dismembered and hidden in various locations, including the cellar and garden of the Wests' home.

* The Wests' home at Cromwell Street became known as the "House of Horrors" after the extent of their crimes was uncovered.

* Some of the victims were found buried in the garden of the Wests' home, while others were discovered in nearby woods and fields.

* The Wests would sometimes invite friends and family to their home while the bodies of their victims were hidden in plain sight, demonstrating their callousness and lack of remorse.

* The Wests' children, including their own offspring and stepchildren, were subjected to physical and sexual abuse, often witnessing the violence inflicted upon the victims.

* Fred West had a history of necrophilia, and he would often engage in sexual acts with the bodies of his victims after their deaths.

* The Wests used their home as a place for violent sexual fantasies and acted out their sadistic desires on their victims.

* The Wests would sometimes drug their victims before assaulting and killing them, further adding to the horror of their crimes.

* Rose West actively participated in the murders, often assisting her husband in the torture and killing of their victims.

* The Wests' crimes went undetected for many years, with neighbors and acquaintances unaware of the horrors unfolding behind closed doors.

* In 1994, their crimes were finally uncovered when one of their daughters revealed the abuse she and her siblings had endured, leading to the police investigation.

* The police found evidence of bloodstains, body parts, and implements of torture, including whips and restraints, in the Wests' home.

* The Wests initially denied the charges against them, but eventually Fred confessed to several murders while Rose maintained her innocence.

* Fred West took his own life by hanging in his jail cell in 1995, leaving Rose as the sole surviving perpetrator of their crimes.

* Rose West was convicted of 10 counts of murder and sentenced to life in prison without the possibility of parole, becoming one of the few women in British history to receive a whole-life tariff.

* Rose West has never shown remorse for her actions and has refused to reveal the full extent of her involvement in the murders.

* Some of the Wests' victims remain unidentified to this day, as the couple's heinous acts left many families without closure.

* The case has also raised questions about how the Wests were able to commit their heinous crimes for so long without detection, exposing flaws in the criminal justice system and social services.

* The Wests' case has also shed light on the issue of domestic violence and the dangers of abusive relationships, as Rose West was a victim of Fred's violence before becoming his accomplice.

* The Wests' home at Cromwell Street was demolished in 1996, and the site has since become a place of infamy and morbid curiosity for true crime enthusiasts.

* It is believed that Fred and Rose West may have had more victims than those they were convicted of killing, as evidence suggests their crimes may have spanned several decades.

Javed Iqbal
Killer of 100 Boys

Javed Iqbal was a Pakistani serial killer who confessed to the murders of at least 100 boys between the ages of 6 and 16, making him one of the most prolific killers in Pakistan's history. Born in 1956 in Lahore, Iqbal had a troubled childhood, marked by abuse from his father and a traumatic experience with a female prostitute, which he claimed had deeply affected his mental state and fueled his desire to kill.

Iqbal's modus operandi involved luring vulnerable boys with promises of food, shelter, or money, and then subjecting them to horrific acts of sexual assault and murder. He would then dismember their bodies and dispose of their remains in vats of acid at his home in Lahore, attempting to erase all evidence of his heinous crimes.

The full extent of Iqbal's crimes came to light in December 1999 when he sent a letter to the police, confessing to the murders and providing gruesome details about the locations where he had dumped the bodies. The letter shocked and horrified the nation, as the sheer number of victims and the brutality of the killings sent shockwaves through the community.

Iqbal was arrested and charged with multiple counts of murder. Initially, he pleaded guilty to all 100 charges, but later retracted his confession, claiming he had been coerced into it. He went through multiple trials and legal proceedings, and his case garnered significant media attention in Pakistan and beyond.

Despite his attempts to recant his confession, Iqbal was found guilty and sentenced to death by hanging in October 2000. However, before the sentence could be carried out, he was found dead in his prison cell in March 2001, having apparently committed suicide by hanging himself with a sheet.

FACT FILE:

❖ Javed Iqbal was born in 1956 in Lahore, Pakistan.

❖ He was known to have a troubled childhood and a history of mental illness.

❖ Iqbal claimed that his abusive father and a traumatic experience with a female prostitute fueled his desire to kill.

❖ He lured his victims, boys between the ages of 6 and 16, with promises of food, shelter, or money.

❖ Iqbal sexually assaulted and brutally murdered his victims, often strangling them to death.

❖ He would then dismember their bodies and dispose of their remains in vats of acid at his home in Lahore.

❖ Iqbal's modus operandi was premeditated and calculated, showing a high degree of planning and organization.

❖ He confessed to the murders in a letter he sent to the police in December 1999, revealing gruesome details about the locations where he had dumped the bodies.

* Iqbal's confession shocked the nation, as the scale and brutality of his crimes were unprecedented in Pakistan's history.

* He claimed to have killed at least 100 boys, making him one of the most prolific serial killers in the country.

* Iqbal's murders were motivated by his depraved desires and lust for power and control over vulnerable victims.

* He showed no remorse for his actions and demonstrated a callous disregard for human life.

* Iqbal's case led to widespread fear and mistrust in the community, as parents and children alike were horrified by the magnitude of his crimes.

* His actions were considered a grave violation of basic human rights and caused significant psychological trauma to the victims' families.

* Iqbal's trial was highly publicized, with media coverage both in Pakistan and internationally.

* He initially pleaded guilty to all 100 charges, but later retracted his confession, claiming he had been coerced into it.

* The case raised questions about the reliability of confessions obtained through interrogation methods in Pakistan's criminal justice system.

* Iqbal's mental state was a subject of debate during the trial, with his defense claiming that he was not mentally sound.

* Despite his attempts to recant his confession, Iqbal was found guilty and sentenced to death by hanging.

* He was incarcerated in a high-security prison, but managed to commit suicide by hanging himself with a sheet in March 2001, before the sentence could be carried out.

* Iqbal's suicide left many unanswered questions and prevented the full extent of justice from being served.

* His case remains one of the most heinous and shocking in Pakistan's history, with a lasting impact on the victims' families and the community.

* The magnitude and brutality of Iqbal's crimes continue to be a subject of morbid fascination and horror for many.

* His crimes shattered the illusion of safety and security, instilling fear and mistrust in the community.

Ian Brady & Myra Hindley

The Moors Murderers

Ian Brady was born in Glasgow, Scotland in 1938. He had a troubled childhood and showed early signs of psychopathy. As a teenager, he developed a fascination with sadistic acts and expressed a desire to commit murder.

Myra Hindley was born in Manchester, England in 1942. She grew up in a working-class family and had a difficult upbringing, often facing bullying and poverty. She met Ian Brady when she was 18 years old, and they formed a sinister bond.

In 1963, the couple embarked on a killing spree that would haunt the nation for years to come. They lured and murdered five children and teenagers, burying their bodies in desolate areas, including Saddleworth Moor. The victims,

Pauline Reade, John Kilbride, Keith Bennett, Lesley Ann Downey, and Edward Evans, were brutally tortured and sexually assaulted before being murdered.

The chilling nature of their crimes shocked the public and left an indelible mark on the history of crime. Brady and Hindley showed no remorse for their actions and displayed a callous disregard for human life. They were convicted of multiple counts of murder and received life imprisonment.

The case of Brady and Hindley was marked by the twisted dynamics of their relationship, with Brady being the dominant and controlling figure, and Hindley often compliant and complicit in his actions. Their crimes were seen as a macabre expression of their depravity and shared fascination with violence.

In the years that followed their convictions, Brady and Hindley became infamous figures in the UK, with their names synonymous with evil. They never revealed the location of Keith Bennett's body, despite numerous appeals from the victim's family, adding to the chilling mystery surrounding their crimes.

Ian Brady died in 2017 in a high-security psychiatric hospital, taking the secrets of their crimes to the grave. Myra Hindley died in 2002, still serving her life sentence, and remained a reviled figure in the eyes of the public.

FACT FILE:

* Ian Brady was born in Glasgow, Scotland in 1938, while Myra Hindley was born in Manchester, England in 1942.

* Ian Brady had a troubled childhood and showed signs of psychopathy as a teenager.

* Myra Hindley grew up in a working-class family and faced bullying and poverty.

* The couple met when Myra was 18 years old, and they formed a sinister bond.

* In 1963, Ian and Myra embarked on a killing spree that lasted for over a year.

* They lured five children and teenagers, sexually assaulted them, and brutally murdered them.

* The couple buried the bodies of their victims in desolate areas, including Saddleworth Moor.

* Ian Brady had a fascination with sadistic acts and expressed a desire to commit murder as a teenager.

* Myra Hindley was often compliant and complicit in Ian Brady's actions, although the dynamics of their relationship were complex and twisted.

* The couple's crimes were seen as a macabre expression of their depravity and shared fascination with violence.

* Ian Brady's signature weapon was a German-made Luger pistol that he had stolen from a soldier's locker.

* Myra Hindley helped to lure Lesley Ann Downey, her youngest victim, by pretending to be lost and asking for help.

* The couple's relationship was marked by sexual sadism, with the victims being subjected to torture and sexual abuse before being murdered.

* Ian Brady was known to have a fascination with Nazi Germany and its ideology.

* The couple was convicted of multiple counts of murder and received life imprisonment.

* Ian Brady was diagnosed with paranoid schizophrenia in 1985 and spent the rest of his life in a high-security psychiatric hospital.

* Myra Hindley was diagnosed with borderline personality disorder and remained in prison until her death in 2002.

* The case of Ian Brady and Myra Hindley is often referred to as the Moors Murders, due to the location where they buried their victims.

* The couple's crimes were seen as a shocking betrayal of trust, as they lured their victims with promises of help or assistance.

* The families of the victims were left devastated by the senseless murders and the lack of remorse shown by the killers.

* Ian Brady's death in 2017 marked the end of the investigation into the Moors Murders.

* Myra Hindley made numerous appeals for parole, but they were all rejected.

* The couple's trial was one of the most sensational in British history, with widespread media coverage and public outcry.

* The story of Ian Brady and Myra Hindley has inspired books, films, and documentaries, and continues to captivate public interest to this day.

* Despite numerous appeals, Ian Brady never revealed the location of Keith Bennett's body, adding to the anguish of the victim's family.

* Myra Hindley's death did not bring closure to the families of the victims, who were left with the enduring trauma of their loved ones' senseless murders.

Joseph DeAngelo
The Golden State Killer

Joseph DeAngelo, also known as the Golden State Killer, is a former police officer and serial killer who terrorized California during the 1970s and 1980s. Born on November 8, 1945, in Bath, New York, DeAngelo grew up in a middle-class family and had a seemingly normal childhood. However, behind his unassuming façade, DeAngelo harbored dark and violent impulses.

In 1973, DeAngelo began his crime spree, committing a series of burglaries, rapes, and murders in California. He targeted suburban neighborhoods, often stalking his victims for weeks or months before attacking them. DeAngelo's methods were meticulous and brutal. He would break into homes at night, wearing a ski mask or other disguise, and would often tie up and gag his victims before subjecting them to sexual assault and other forms of torture.

DeAngelo's crimes escalated over time, earning him the moniker of the Golden State Killer. He committed at least 13 known murders and more than 50 rapes, as well as numerous burglaries, during his reign of terror. His ability to evade capture for decades earned him a reputation as a cunning and elusive predator.

Despite extensive efforts by law enforcement to catch the Golden State Killer, DeAngelo remained at large for over 40 years. However, in 2018, advancements in DNA technology led to his arrest. DeAngelo was finally identified as the Golden State Killer and was subsequently charged with multiple counts of murder and other crimes.

In a chilling revelation, it was discovered that DeAngelo had been living a double life, appearing as a normal family man while secretly committing heinous crimes. His ability to blend into society and maintain a façade of normalcy shocked those who knew him.

DeAngelo's trial has been marked by the harrowing testimonies of his victims and their families, who have endured decades of trauma. His chilling biography is a disturbing reminder of the dark and twisted depths that some individuals are capable of, and the lasting impact that serial killers can have on their victims and society as a whole.

FACT FILE:

* Joseph DeAngelo, also known as the "Golden State Killer" and the "East Area Rapist," was born on November 8, 1945, in Bath, New York, USA.

* DeAngelo grew up in a middle-class household and had a relatively normal childhood, showing no early signs of the violent crimes he would later commit.

* He served in the United States Navy during the Vietnam War and later worked as a police officer in various California law enforcement agencies, including the Exeter Police Department and the Auburn Police Department.

* DeAngelo committed a series of burglaries, rapes, and murders across California in the 1970s and 1980s, terrorizing communities and leaving a trail of victims in his wake.

* He was known for his meticulous planning and preparation, often stalking his victims for extended periods of time before attacking them in their homes.

* DeAngelo would often target couples, tying up the male partner and subjecting the female partner to sexual assault, displaying a pattern of sadistic behavior.

* He was known to use elaborate ruses and disguises to gain entry into his victims' homes, including posing as a police officer or wearing a ski mask to conceal his identity.

* DeAngelo was also known for his meticulous clean-up after his crimes, leaving behind few traces of evidence and creating challenges for investigators to link him to the crimes.

* He was initially referred to as the "East Area Rapist" due to his early crimes in the Sacramento area, and later became known as the "Original Night Stalker" as he continued his reign of terror across different regions in California.

* DeAngelo's crimes included at least 13 known murders and numerous rapes and burglaries, though the exact number of his victims may be higher.

* He often taunted his victims and their families, making harassing phone calls and leaving menacing messages at crime scenes, instilling fear and terrorizing the communities.

* DeAngelo used a variety of weapons during his crimes, including handguns, knives, and ligatures, and was known for his brutality and violence towards his victims.

* He frequently changed his modus operandi, adapting his techniques to avoid detection and elude capture, showing a high level of cunning and calculated planning.

* DeAngelo was known to conduct meticulous surveillance on his victims, often stalking them for weeks or even months before attacking, showing a high degree of patience and planning.

* He would sometimes return to the homes of his previous victims, further terrorizing them and demonstrating a sense of sadistic enjoyment in their fear and suffering.

* DeAngelo was known to have a fascination with knots and would often bind his victims using intricate and elaborate ligatures, adding to the chilling nature of his crimes.

* He was also known to steal personal items from his victims, such as jewelry or keepsakes, as trophies or mementos of his crimes.

* DeAngelo's crimes remained unsolved for over four decades, creating a sense of mystery and fear in the communities he targeted.

* He was arrested in April 2018, after investigators used DNA evidence to link him to the crimes, marking a significant breakthrough in the case.

* DeAngelo's arrest shocked the nation and brought closure to many of the victims' families, but also raised questions about how he had evaded capture for so long.

* He pleaded guilty to multiple charges, including murder and kidnapping, and was sentenced to life in prison without the possibility of parole in August 2020.

* It was revealed during his trial that DeAngelo had led a double life, appearing to be a normal family man to those who knew him, while secretly committing heinous crimes.

* DeAngelo had multiple aliases and fake identities that he used to evade detection, including using different names and license plates on his vehicles.

* He would meticulously plan his crimes, often studying maps, conducting surveillance, and selecting victims in advance, showcasing his meticulous and methodical approach to his crimes.

* DeAngelo was known to break into homes and move items around or make small changes to the environment, further fueling the fear and paranoia of his victims.

* He would sometimes leave cryptic messages or clues at crime scenes, taunting law enforcement and the public, and leaving them to speculate about his motives and identity.

- DeAngelo was known to stalk his victims even after the initial attacks, harassing them with threatening phone calls or other means, further instilling fear and terror.

- He often targeted women who were alone or vulnerable, such as those who lived alone or were home alone at the time of the attack, showcasing his predatory behavior.

- DeAngelo's crimes had a long-lasting and profound impact on the survivors, their families, and the communities he terrorized, leaving deep emotional scars that persist to this day.

Harold Shipman
Dr. Death

Harold Shipman, born on January 14, 1946, in Nottingham, England, was a medical doctor and one of the most notorious serial killers in history, known as "Dr. Death." His chilling biography is marked by a long and sinister history of murder, deception, and betrayal.

Shipman's childhood was relatively unremarkable, and he showed an early interest in medicine. He attended Leeds Medical School and went on to work as a general practitioner (GP) in Hyde, Greater Manchester. He built a reputation as a trusted and caring doctor, gaining the confidence of his patients and the respect of his colleagues.

However, behind the façade of a respected physician, Shipman had a dark and twisted secret. Starting in the 1970s and spanning over two decades, he began systematically murdering his patients. He would visit patients in their homes, often targeting vulnerable and elderly individuals, and administer lethal doses of diamorphine, a powerful painkiller. He would then forge medical records to cover up his tracks, creating a web of deceit to conceal his crimes.

Shipman's reign of terror went unnoticed for years, as he carefully selected victims who were unlikely to arouse suspicion. His charming and personable demeanor, along with his medical knowledge and authority, helped him evade detection for a long time. However, in 1998, a fellow doctor became suspicious of the unusually high number of deaths under Shipman's care and alerted the authorities.

Subsequent investigations uncovered a pattern of suspicious deaths and revealed the extent of Shipman's heinous crimes. In January 2000, he was arrested and charged with 15 counts of murder. As the investigation continued, it was believed that Shipman had killed over 250 patients, though the exact number remains unknown.

In January 2004, Shipman was convicted of 15 counts of murder and one count of forgery. He was sentenced to life in prison without the possibility of parole, and he took his own life by hanging in his cell on January 13, 2004, the day before his 58th birthday.

FACT FILE:

* Harold Shipman, also known as "Dr. Death," was a British general practitioner and serial killer who murdered at least 15 and possibly over 250 of his patients.

* Shipman was born on January 14, 1946, in Nottingham, England, and grew up in a middle-class family.

* He attended Leeds Medical School and qualified as a doctor in 1970.

* Shipman began working as a GP in Hyde, Greater Manchester, where he built a reputation as a caring and trusted doctor.

* He targeted elderly patients, primarily women, whom he viewed as vulnerable and less likely to be suspicious.

* Shipman's preferred method of killing was injecting his victims with lethal doses of diamorphine, a powerful painkiller.

* He would often administer the fatal injections in the patient's own home, making it difficult for others to witness or intervene.

* Shipman was skilled at forging medical records to cover up his crimes, creating a false impression of natural causes of death.

* He manipulated the wills of his victims, leaving himself as a beneficiary, and gained financial gain from their deaths.

* Shipman's killing spree lasted for over two decades, from the 1970s to 1998, before he was finally caught.

* He was initially arrested in September 1998 after a colleague became suspicious of the high death rate among Shipman's patients.

* Shipman was charged with 15 counts of murder, but the investigation uncovered evidence of many more potential victims.

* He was known to be arrogant and unemotional, showing no remorse for his actions during his trial.

* Shipman's trial, which began in 1999, was one of the largest in British legal history, involving extensive forensic evidence and testimonies from numerous witnesses.

* He was found guilty of 15 counts of murder and one count of forgery in January 2000 and was sentenced to life in prison without parole.

* Shipman is believed to have been motivated by a thirst for power and control, rather than financial gain.

* He is suspected of having killed over 250 patients, making him one of the most prolific serial killers in history.

* Shipman's crimes had a devastating impact on the families of his victims, who were left grieving and struggling to comprehend the betrayal by their trusted doctor.

* He is known to have forged wills of his victims to inherit their possessions and assets, amassing significant wealth from his murders.

* Shipman's actions shattered the trust in the medical profession and resulted in increased scrutiny of doctors' prescribing practices and patient care.

* He exhibited narcissistic and sociopathic traits, showing a lack of empathy or remorse for the lives he took.

* Shipman's case prompted changes in regulations and oversight of doctors' practices in the United Kingdom, including stricter monitoring and reporting of patient deaths.

* He was known to have a "God complex," believing he had the power of life and death over his patients.

* Shipman's chillingly calculated approach to murder and his ability to deceive his patients, colleagues, and authorities for years shocked the world.

* He was the first British doctor to be found guilty of murdering his patients, making his case a landmark in legal and medical history.

* Shipman's crimes had a significant psychological impact on those involved in the investigation, trial, and aftermath, leaving deep scars on the community and the healthcare profession.

* He is known to have destroyed medical records to cover up his tracks, making it difficult to determine the exact number of his victims.

* Shipman's murders were a grave breach of trust, as he violated the fundamental principle of medical ethics to "do no harm" and instead took advantage of his patients' vulnerabilities for his own gain.

* Shipman's killings were not limited to a specific demographic or background, as he targeted patients of various ages, genders, and socioeconomic statuses, making his crimes even more chilling.

* Shipman's case revealed the potential for abuse of power and manipulation within the healthcare system, highlighting the need for thorough screening, oversight, and accountability of medical professionals.

Earle Nelson
The Gorilla Man

Earle Nelson, known as the "Gorilla Man" or the "Dark Strangler," was an American serial killer who terrorized the United States during the early 20th century. Nelson's chilling acts of violence and brutality shocked the nation, leaving a trail of death and horror in his wake.

Born on May 12, 1897, in San Francisco, California, Nelson had a troubled childhood, marked by a history of abuse and neglect. He grew up in poverty and experienced frequent run-ins with the law, including arrests for theft and assault. However, it was his later actions that would earn him notoriety as one of the most prolific and brutal serial killers in American history.

Nelson's killing spree began in 1926 and lasted until his capture in 1927. He targeted vulnerable women, often posing as a door-to-door salesman or a handyman to gain access to their homes. Once inside, he would viciously attack and strangle his victims, leaving their lifeless bodies behind in a gruesome display of violence.

Nelson's actions were characterized by extreme brutality and sadism. He would often sexually assault his victims and mutilate their bodies after killing them, adding an additional layer of horror to his crimes. His methods were calculated and ruthless, and he showed no remorse for his actions.

During his spree, Nelson traveled across the United States, leaving a trail of death and destruction in multiple states, including California, Illinois, and Canada. He managed to evade capture for a significant period of time, despite the intense efforts of law enforcement to track him down.

However, Nelson's reign of terror came to an end in 1927 when he was finally arrested in Canada after attempting to assault a woman in a hotel. He was subsequently extradited to the United States and stood trial for his heinous crimes.

Nelson's trial was marked by sensationalism and media attention, with the public captivated by the gruesome details of his murders. He was eventually found guilty and sentenced to death by hanging. On January 13, 1928, Nelson was executed in Winnipeg, Canada, bringing an end to his chilling and horrific spree of violence.

FACT FILE:

❖ Earle Nelson was born on May 12, 1897, in San Francisco, California, and grew up in poverty with a history of abuse and neglect.

❖ Nelson's killing spree began in 1926 and lasted until his capture in 1927, during which he targeted vulnerable women across the United States and Canada.

❖ He was known as the "Gorilla Man" or the "Dark Strangler" due to his physical strength and violent methods of strangulation.

❖ Nelson would often pose as a door-to-door salesman or a handyman to gain access to his victims' homes, where he would then brutally attack and strangle them.

❖ He sexually assaulted many of his victims and often mutilated their bodies after killing them, displaying a high level of sadism and brutality.

❖ Nelson was known to move frequently, often changing his name and using aliases to evade capture and continue his killing spree.

❖ He was known to prey on elderly women, young girls, and those living alone, taking advantage of their vulnerability.

* Nelson's spree of violence spanned multiple states in the United States, including California, Illinois, and multiple provinces in Canada.

* He would often leave his victims' bodies in gruesome and degrading positions, adding an additional level of horror to his crimes.

* Nelson was known to be extremely cunning and elusive, managing to evade capture for an extended period of time despite intense efforts by law enforcement to track him down.

* He was arrested in Canada in 1927 after attempting to assault a woman in a hotel, leading to his extradition to the United States for trial.

* Nelson's trial was marked by sensationalism and media attention, with the public captivated by the gruesome details of his murders.

* During his trial, it was revealed that Nelson had a history of mental illness and had been institutionalized in the past.

* He was found guilty of multiple counts of murder and sentenced to death by hanging.

* Nelson showed no remorse for his actions during his trial and remained unrepentant until his execution.

* He was executed by hanging on January 13, 1928, in Winnipeg, Canada.

* Nelson's chilling and horrific spree of violence left a lasting impact on the communities and families of his victims.

* He is believed to have killed at least 22 women, although the actual number of his victims may be higher.

* Nelson's modus operandi of strangulation and mutilation earned him a reputation as one of the most sadistic and brutal serial killers in American history.

* He was known to have an intense hatred towards women, which fueled his violent acts.

* Nelson had a pattern of stalking and preying on his victims, carefully selecting vulnerable individuals whom he believed would be easy targets.

* He often traveled by train, using it as a means to move from place to place and evade capture.

* Nelson's killings were marked by a high degree of premeditation and planning, indicating a cold and calculating nature.

* He had a history of violence and criminal behavior prior to his killing spree, including arrests for theft and assault.

* Nelson's actions sent shockwaves through the communities where his crimes were committed, instilling fear and paranoia among residents.

* He was known to have a manipulative and charming personality, which he used to gain the trust of his victims and gain access to their homes.

* Nelson's murders were often committed in a ritualistic manner, with specific patterns and methods that he followed.

* He had a history of evading capture and escaping from custody, displaying a high level of cunning and resourcefulness.

* Nelson's killings were characterized by a high level of brutality and sadism, with evidence of extreme violence and mutilation inflicted upon his victims.

Dorothea Puente
The Death House Landlady

Dorothea Puente was an American serial killer who operated in Sacramento, California, during the 1980s. Born on January 9, 1929, in Redlands, California, Puente had a troubled upbringing and a history of criminal activities. However, it wasn't until her later years that she would become notorious for her chilling crimes.

Puente ran a boarding house for elderly and disabled individuals in Sacramento, where she would later carry out her murderous deeds. She was known for her charming and charismatic demeanor, which helped her gain the trust of vulnerable residents who sought shelter at her boarding house. However, beneath her facade of kindness, Puente harbored dark and sinister motives.

Between the years 1982 and 1988, Puente lured at least nine of her elderly tenants to their deaths. She would drug her victims with lethal doses of prescription medications, then bury their bodies in the backyard of her boarding house. She would then cash their Social Security checks and forge their signatures to steal their money.

Puente's crimes were discovered in 1988 when a social worker became suspicious of her activities and alerted the authorities. Upon investigation, the bodies of seven of her victims were unearthed from the backyard of her boarding house. Puente was arrested and charged with murder.

During her trial, Puente showed no remorse and even tried to represent herself in court. She was found guilty of three counts of first-degree murder and six counts of second-degree murder, and was sentenced to life in prison without the possibility of parole.

Throughout her incarceration, Puente maintained her innocence, claiming that she was framed by others. However, the chilling details of her crimes, including the exploitation of vulnerable elderly individuals for financial gain, painted a disturbing picture of a calculating and heartless killer.

Dorothea Puente died in prison on March 27, 2011, at the age of 82. Her chilling crimes and the horrific exploitation of her victims continue to haunt those who remember her heinous acts.

FACT FILE:

* Dorothea Puente was born in 1929 in Redlands, California, and grew up in a troubled household with a history of criminal activities.

* She was married and divorced four times and had several run-ins with the law for fraud, forgery, and theft.

* In the early 1980s, Puente started running a boarding house for elderly and disabled individuals in Sacramento, California.

* She was known for her charming and charismatic personality and would lure her victims by offering them a place to stay and care.

* Puente would drug her victims with prescription medications, then kill them and bury their bodies in the backyard of her boarding house.

* She would then cash their Social Security checks and steal their money.

* Puente was suspected of killing her first victim, Ruth Munroe, in 1982. However, she was not charged with her murder.

* Over the next few years, Puente would kill at least eight more of her tenants, making her one of the most prolific female serial killers in American history.

* She would alter the Social Security checks of her victims, forging their signatures to make it appear as if they were still alive.

* Puente had several aliases, including "Death House Landlady," "Lady Blue Beard," and "The Black Widow of Sacramento."

* She had a close relationship with local law enforcement officers, who had been known to turn a blind eye to her activities.

* Puente was finally caught in 1988 when a social worker became suspicious of her and alerted the authorities.

* When police searched her boarding house, they found the bodies of seven of her victims buried in the backyard.

* Puente was arrested and charged with multiple counts of murder, forgery, and theft.

* During her trial, Puente claimed that she was innocent and had been framed by others.

* She also attempted to represent herself in court but was ultimately found guilty of three counts of first-degree murder and six counts of second-degree murder.

* Puente was sentenced to life in prison without the possibility of parole.

* Despite her conviction, Puente maintained her innocence throughout her life.

* She was known to have written letters to friends and acquaintances, expressing her desire to be released from prison and seeking support for her cause.

* Puente was diagnosed with dementia and other health issues while in prison and was often confined to a wheelchair.

* In 2011, Puente died in prison at the age of 82.

* After her death, her belongings were auctioned off, and her personal items, including her clothing and jewelry, were sold for thousands of dollars.

* Puente's boarding house, located on F Street in Sacramento, has since been demolished, and the property has been turned into a memorial garden for her victims.

* Puente's boarding house was found to have been in deplorable conditions, with evidence of neglect and mistreatment of her tenants.

* She was known to have used various aliases and false identities to avoid detection and continue her criminal activities.

* Puente had a history of mental health issues, including bipolar disorder and depression, which may have played a role in her violent behavior.

* She had a fascination with death and was known to have visited graveyards and attended funerals, possibly indicating a morbid obsession.

* Puente's crimes were carefully planned and executed, showing a high level of premeditation and cunning.

* She manipulated her victims' families and friends, pretending to be caring and concerned while secretly profiting from their deaths.

* She remains one of the most notorious female serial killers in history.

Dennis Rader

The BTK Killer

Dennis Rader, also known as the "BTK Killer," was an American serial killer who terrorized the community of Wichita, Kansas, from the 1970s to the 1980s. Born on March 9, 1945, in Pittsburg, Kansas, Rader led a seemingly normal life as a family man, churchgoer, and local government employee. However, beneath his seemingly benign facade, Rader harbored a dark and twisted obsession with murder.

Rader's first known murder occurred in 1974 when he killed four members of the Otero family, including two young children. He went on to commit a series of brutal and sadistic killings over the years, taunting law enforcement and the media with cryptic messages and letters, which earned him the moniker "BTK" for his modus operandi of binding, torturing, and killing his victims.

Rader's killings were meticulously planned and executed. He would stalk his victims, often breaking into their homes to gather information about their routines and habits. He would then strike, binding, torturing, and killing his victims in cold blood. Rader's victims included men, women, and children, and he showed no remorse for his heinous crimes.

Rader's reign of terror lasted for decades, during which he sent letters and packages to the media and law enforcement, boasting about his killings and leaving clues to taunt them. However, Rader's arrogance ultimately led to his downfall when he sent a floppy disk to the police in 2004, which was traced back to a computer at his church. He was subsequently arrested and pleaded guilty to 10 counts of first-degree murder.

Dennis Rader was sentenced to 10 consecutive life sentences without the possibility of parole. His chilling crimes and lack of remorse continue to haunt the victims' families and the community to this day. Rader's case remains one of the most notorious and disturbing in the annals of American criminal history, serving as a stark reminder of the capacity for evil that can lurk in the most unexpected places.

FACT FILE:

* Dennis Rader, also known as the "BTK Killer," stands for "Bind, Torture, Kill," which was his signature in describing his brutal and sadistic murders.

* Rader killed ten people between 1974 and 1991 in Wichita, Kansas, with a particular focus on targeting women.

* He sent taunting letters to the police and local media, describing the details of his murders and claiming responsibility for them.

* Rader's killings were carefully planned and executed, with a high level of sadistic violence and sexual gratification derived from the torture and murder of his victims.

* He often stalked his victims, studying their habits and routines before striking, which added to the terror and fear among the local community.

* Rader had a fetish for bondage, and he would often restrain and torture his victims before killing them.

* He took great pleasure in taunting and terrorizing his victims, often playing psychological games with them before ultimately ending their lives.

* Rader had a "normal" family life, with a wife and children, which made his double life as a serial killer all the more chilling and disturbing.

* He meticulously planned his murders, selecting victims and locations carefully to avoid detection, and often revisited the crime scenes to relive the killings.

* Rader was known to have taken souvenirs from his victims, including personal belongings and mementos, which he kept as trophies.

* He showed a complete lack of empathy or remorse for his actions, often referring to his victims in derogatory terms and showing no remorse for their brutal deaths.

* Rader's killings were characterized by extreme violence, including strangulation, stabbing, and mutilation, leaving a trail of brutalized bodies in his wake.

* He engaged in a cat-and-mouse game with law enforcement and the media, sending cryptic messages and clues in his letters, which added to the fear and mystique surrounding his case.

* Rader was known to have a deep fascination with his own notoriety and craved attention, often seeking recognition and praise for his heinous acts.

* He showed a high degree of cunning and intelligence in avoiding capture for many years, eluding law enforcement and leaving them baffled by his elusive nature.

* Rader carefully planned his crimes, often conducting surveillance on his victims for extended periods of time, waiting for the perfect moment to strike.

* He had a detailed knowledge of law enforcement procedures and forensic techniques, which he used to his advantage in evading capture for so long.

* Rader had a sadistic and narcissistic personality, deriving pleasure from the suffering and terror he inflicted on his victims and the community.

* He engaged in risky behavior, such as sending letters and clues to the media and law enforcement, taunting them and challenging them to catch him.

* Rader's case was one of the most notorious and perplexing in the history of serial killers, with his ability to evade capture for so long and his cold, calculated manner of killing.

* Rader kept a detailed journal in which he documented his thoughts, fantasies, and plans for future murders, providing chilling insight into his twisted mind.

* He targeted his victims based on a variety of factors, including their appearance, occupation, and proximity to his home, displaying a high level of calculated planning and stalking.

* Rader often engaged in "reconnaissance missions" prior to his killings, breaking into the homes of his victims and collecting information about their routines and habits.

* He had a penchant for staging his crime scenes, arranging the bodies of his victims in grotesque poses and leaving clues to taunt law enforcement and instill fear in the community.

Carroll Cole

The Strangler

Carroll Edward Cole was born on May 9, 1939, in Sioux City, Iowa, to a family that was characterized by a history of violence, addiction, and mental illness. His father, Glen Cole, was an alcoholic who physically abused him, his siblings, and their mother, Grace. Carroll Cole's mother was an overbearing and domineering figure who often belittled and humiliated her children.

Cole's childhood was marked by a series of traumatic experiences that likely contributed to his later descent into violence. At the age of five, he suffered from a bout of encephalitis that left him with a severe stutter and difficulty speaking. As a result, he was often bullied and teased by his peers, which further compounded his feelings of isolation and alienation.

Despite these challenges, Cole excelled academically and went on to attend college, where he earned a degree in electrical engineering. However, his success was short-lived, and he eventually dropped out of school and began to drift from one job to another.

Cole's first known murder occurred in 1948, when he was just 19 years old. He had been dating a young girl named Marlene Walters, but when she threatened to reveal their relationship to his family, he strangled her to death and buried her body in a shallow grave. He went on to commit a series of brutal murders of women in the 1960s and 1970s, targeting vulnerable individuals, including sex workers and hitchhikers.

Cole's modus operandi involved luring his victims to secluded areas, where he would sexually assault and murder them. He would then mutilate their bodies and dispose of them in remote locations, often leaving them in gruesome and disturbing states. Cole's killings were characterized by a lack of remorse or empathy for his victims. He showed a callous disregard for human life and was known to have confessed to his crimes without showing any signs of guilt or remorse.

Cole's murderous spree came to an end in 1980 when he was arrested and eventually convicted for multiple counts of murder. He was sentenced to death for his heinous crimes and was executed by lethal injection on December 6, 1985.

FACT FILE:

❖ Carroll Cole confessed to killing 13 people, although he claimed to have killed over 35, making him one of the most prolific serial killers in American history.

❖ Cole's victims were predominantly young women, including sex workers and hitchhikers, whom he targeted for his heinous acts.

❖ He was known for sexually assaulting and mutilating the bodies of his victims, leaving them in gruesome and disturbing states.

❖ Cole's first known murder was committed when he was just 19 years old, and he continued to kill for over two decades.

❖ He often used different aliases and changed his appearance to avoid detection, making it difficult for law enforcement to connect the dots and identify him as a serial killer.

❖ He claimed to have suffered from multiple personalities and to have been possessed by demons at the time of his crimes, adding an eerie and chilling dimension to his actions.

* Cole had a history of violence and abuse in his family, with his father being an alcoholic who physically abused him and his siblings, and his mother being overbearing and domineering.

* He often buried his victims in remote locations, making it difficult for authorities to locate their bodies and bring him to justice.

* Cole's killings were characterized by a cold, calculating, and methodical approach, carefully selecting and targeting vulnerable victims.

* He had a history of failed relationships, divorces, and difficulties with intimacy, which may have contributed to his violent behavior.

* Cole was known to have been charming and manipulative, able to blend in with his surroundings and appear normal to those around him.

* He had a fascination with death and reportedly kept souvenirs from his victims, including personal belongings and body parts.

* Cole's crimes shocked the communities where he lived and operated, creating fear and paranoia among local residents.

* He evaded capture for years, changing locations and avoiding detection, which added to the mystery and fear surrounding his crimes.

* Cole's childhood was marked by traumatic experiences, including a bout of encephalitis that left him with a severe stutter and difficulty speaking, and being bullied and teased by his peers.

* He was known to have a volatile temper and a history of violent outbursts, both as a child and an adult.

* Cole's confessions and statements about his motivations were often contradictory and confusing, adding to the chilling nature of his personality.

* He had a history of mental health issues, including claims of multiple personalities and demonic possession, which raised questions about his sanity and culpability.

* He was sentenced to death for his crimes and was executed by lethal injection, bringing an end to his reign of terror.

* Cole's case has been extensively studied by criminologists and forensic psychologists, adding to our understanding of the psychology and motivations of serial killers.

* He manipulated and deceived those around him, including law enforcement, which contributed to his ability to evade capture for so long.

* Cole's gruesome acts and lack of remorse continue to send chills down the spine of those who study or hear about his case.

* He left a trail of horror and fear in the communities where he lived and operated, leaving a lasting legacy of terror.

Carl Panzram
Gray Eyed Killer

Carl Panzram was born on June 28, 1891, in Warren, Minnesota, USA. He had a troubled childhood marked by abuse, neglect, and instability. His father abandoned the family, and his mother remarried multiple times, exposing Panzram to a series of abusive stepfathers. As a result, Panzram grew up with deep-seated anger, resentment, and a propensity for violence.

Panzram's early life was marred by a long history of criminal behavior. He ran away from home at a young age, engaging in theft, burglary, and arson. He was arrested for the first time at the age of 8 for stealing and was subsequently placed in various reform schools and juvenile detention centers, which only fueled his resentment towards authority figures.

As he grew older, Panzram's criminal activities escalated to more heinous acts. He became known for his brutal and sadistic nature, preying on vulnerable individuals, particularly young boys and men. He would often lure them into isolated areas with promises of work or money, only to violently assault and kill them. Panzram showed no mercy or remorse, often mutilating and torturing his victims before taking their lives.

Panzram's violent tendencies continued to escalate, and he left a trail of terror across multiple states in the United States. He would frequently change his appearance, use fake names, and travel extensively to avoid detection by law enforcement. He was known to have committed multiple murders, rapes, and acts of arson, leaving a path of destruction in his wake.

Panzram's criminal activities eventually caught up with him, and he was apprehended in 1928 after attempting to steal a yacht in California. He was subsequently convicted of various crimes, including murder, arson, and sodomy, and was sentenced to prison. However, his violent behavior did not cease even in prison, as he frequently attacked fellow inmates and staff, earning a reputation as a dangerous and uncontrollable inmate.

Despite multiple escape attempts and acts of violence, Panzram was eventually executed by hanging on September 5, 1930, at the age of 39. His chilling legacy as a ruthless and sadistic serial killer lives on.

FACT FILE:

* Carl Panzram claimed to have committed over 20 murders, as well as numerous acts of rape, arson, and other violent crimes.

* Panzram's first known murder was committed when he was just 11 years old, when he pushed a man off a moving train.

* He was arrested for the first time at the age of 8 for stealing and was placed in various reform schools and juvenile detention centers.

* Panzram served multiple prison sentences throughout his life, including time in notorious prisons such as Leavenworth and San Quentin.

* While in prison, Panzram was known for his violent behavior, frequently attacking fellow inmates and prison staff.

* Panzram once wrote in his autobiography, "I wish all mankind had one neck, and I had my hands around it."

* He claimed to have sodomized over 1,000 males, including children and adults, and expressed no remorse for his actions.

* Panzram once set fire to a church, causing extensive damage, and later boasted about it in his autobiography.

* He referred to himself as a "human wolf" and showed a complete lack of empathy or remorse for his victims.

* Panzram used various aliases and changed his appearance frequently to avoid detection by law enforcement.

* He was known to have targeted vulnerable individuals, such as young boys and homeless men, whom he would lure into isolated areas before attacking them.

* Panzram once wrote in his autobiography, "In my lifetime I have murdered 21 human beings, I have committed thousands of burglaries, robberies, larcenies, arsons and, last but not least, I have committed sodomy on more than 1,000 male human beings."

* He claimed to have killed a man with his bare hands and once boasted that he could "kill a man quicker than anyone who's ever lived."

* Panzram attempted to escape from prison multiple times, showing his persistent and determined nature.

* He once threatened to kill a prison warden and was known to have made several attempts on the lives of prison staff.

* Panzram's acts of violence and depravity were not limited to the United States, as he also committed crimes in Africa and other countries while traveling.

* He mutilated and tortured his victims, showing a sadistic and cruel streak in his actions.

* Panzram once said in an interview, "I don't believe in man, God nor devil. I hate the whole damned human race, including myself."

* He once attempted to commit suicide by slashing his own throat while in prison, but he survived the attempt.

* Panzram was known for his lack of remorse, often stating that he was proud of his crimes and would kill again if given the chance.

* Panzram's crimes spanned over multiple decades, with his first known murder occurring in 1903 and his last known murder in 1928.

* He once claimed to have killed a man just for the thrill of it, stating that he derived pleasure from the act of taking a life.

* Panzram's hatred towards humanity extended to animals as well, as he killed and mutilated animals in his youth.

* He was known to have engaged in necrophilia, mutilating the bodies of his victims after killing them.

* He was known to have targeted vulnerable individuals, such as hitchhikers and homeless people, whom he viewed as easy prey.

* Panzram once stated that he would "like to go to hell, just for the company" and expressed a complete disregard for moral and societal norms.

* Panzram died by execution in the gas chamber at the age of 39, showing no remorse or regret for his heinous crimes even in his final moments.

Carl Eugene Watts

The Sunday Morning Slasher

Carl Eugene Watts, also known as "The Sunday Morning Slasher" and "The Michigan Murderer," was an American serial killer who terrorized communities in Michigan and Texas during the 1970s and 1980s. Born on November 7, 1953, in Killeen, Texas, Watts showed early signs of behavioral problems and was known to have a troubled childhood.

As a teenager, Watts began to exhibit violent and predatory tendencies, and he was known to have a fascination with fire and animals. He dropped out of high school and began drifting across different states, committing a series of burglaries, assaults, and other crimes along the way.

Watts' killing spree began in 1974 when he moved to Michigan and started targeting women, mostly young

African-American females. He would often break into their homes, brutally assault and murder them, and then disappear without a trace. Watts was known to have a pattern of choosing his victims at random, often attacking them in the early hours of Sunday mornings, hence the nickname "The Sunday Morning Slasher."

One of the chilling aspects of Watts' crimes was his ability to blend in with society, appearing to be a normal and unassuming individual. He was known to have a charming and charismatic personality, which he used to gain the trust of his victims and manipulate them into vulnerable situations.

Watts' killing spree continued for several years, during which he moved to Texas and continued his reign of terror. He is believed to have killed at least 13 women, although the actual number of his victims may never be known. He was finally caught in 1982 when he attacked a woman in Texas, but she managed to escape and report him to the police.

After his arrest, Watts confessed to multiple murders, although he often gave conflicting accounts and details of his crimes. He was eventually convicted of several murders and sentenced to life in prison without the possibility of parole. Watts died of prostate cancer in prison on September 21, 2007, taking the full extent of his heinous crimes to his grave. His case remains one of the most chilling and baffling in the history of American serial killers, as the full scope of his brutality and the true number of his victims may never be fully known.

FACT FILE:

* Watts confessed to murdering at least 13 women, but it is believed that the actual number of his victims may be much higher.

* He was known as "The Sunday Morning Slasher" due to his pattern of attacking and killing women on Sunday mornings.

* Watts often gained entry into his victims' homes by posing as a maintenance worker or repairman.

* He targeted young, African-American females, often attacking them while they were asleep in their homes.

* He would brutally assault and strangle his victims, often leaving evidence of sexual assault at the crime scenes.

* Watts was known to have a fascination with fire and would sometimes set fires after committing his murders.

* He was skilled at evading detection, often leaving no physical evidence behind and changing his modus operandi to avoid suspicion.

* Watts traveled across multiple states, committing crimes in Michigan and Texas, making it difficult for law enforcement to track his movements.

* He often stalked his victims for extended periods of time, carefully planning his attacks.

* Watts sometimes posed the bodies of his victims after their deaths, arranging them in specific positions.

* He had a history of violence and had been arrested for assault and burglary before he began his killing spree.

* Watts was known to have a troubled childhood, displaying behavioral problems and signs of aggression from an early age.

* Watts was able to blend in with society and appeared to be a normal and unassuming individual, which helped him evade suspicion.

* He often followed news coverage of his crimes and took pleasure in seeing the fear and panic they caused.

* Watts once said in an interview that killing gave him a "high" and that he enjoyed the feeling of power and control it gave him.

* He admitted to having sadistic and violent fantasies, which he acted out on his victims.
* Watts was known to have a history of failed relationships and difficulty forming meaningful connections with others.

* He once stated that he believed he was doing his victims a favor by killing them, as he believed it would prevent them from experiencing future suffering.

* Watts sometimes returned to the scenes of his crimes to relive the murders and taunt law enforcement.

* He often used different aliases and fake names to avoid detection and cover his tracks.

* Watts was known to have a fascination with weapons, and he used various tools and weapons in his attacks.

* He was known to have a temper and would become easily agitated and violent when provoked.

* Watts was able to avoid suspicion for many years, and it wasn't until a failed attack in Texas that he was finally caught.

* He initially pleaded not guilty by reason of insanity, but later changed his plea to guilty.

* He was sentenced to life in prison without the possibility of parole for his murders.

* Watts died of prostate cancer in prison on September 21, 2007, at the age of 53.

Arthur Shawcross

The Genesee River Killer

Arthur Shawcross was born on June 6, 1945, in Kittery, Maine, USA, and grew up in a troubled household marked by domestic violence and abuse. As a child, he exhibited a pattern of cruelty towards animals and was known to set fires, foreshadowing the darkness that would later consume him.

Shawcross enlisted in the U.S. Army and served in Vietnam, where he claimed to have committed atrocities and developed a taste for violence. After his military service, he struggled with a troubled personal life, including failed marriages and a history of criminal behavior, including theft and arson.

In 1988, Shawcross began a reign of terror as a serial killer. He preyed on vulnerable women, particularly prostitutes and sex workers, in and around Rochester, New York. He would often strangle his victims and mutilate their bodies, leaving a trail of mutilation and carnage in his wake.

Shawcross evaded capture for several years, skillfully covering his tracks and blending into society. He would taunt law enforcement with letters and phone calls, playing a cat-and-mouse game with investigators. He was known to change his appearance and use aliases to avoid suspicion.

In 1990, Shawcross was finally apprehended after he was caught dumping the body of one of his victims. He confessed to a series of brutal murders, claiming that he derived pleasure from the act of killing and mutilating his victims. He showed a chilling lack of remorse and described his crimes in graphic and gruesome detail.

During his trial, Shawcross displayed a chilling demeanor, often smiling and making obscene gestures to the media and the families of his victims. He was convicted of 11 counts of murder and sentenced to life in prison without parole.

FACT FILE:

* Arthur Shawcross, known as the "Genesee River Killer," was convicted of murdering 11 people, mostly women, in the Rochester, New York area during the late 1980s and early 1990s.

* Shawcross had a history of violence and cruelty towards animals, often torturing and killing them as a child, which is considered a common early indicator of psychopathic behavior.

* He claimed to have committed atrocities during his time in the U.S. Army during the Vietnam War, which may have contributed to his later violent behavior.

* Shawcross was known for his brutality, often strangling his victims and mutilating their bodies post-mortem. He would sometimes remove body parts and take them as trophies.

* He targeted vulnerable women, particularly prostitutes and sex workers, whom he believed would be less likely to be missed or investigated by law enforcement.

* Shawcross had a history of criminal behavior, including theft, arson, and assault, even prior to his serial killing spree.

* He had a talent for evading capture, often changing his appearance, using aliases, and manipulating law enforcement to avoid suspicion.

* Shawcross would taunt law enforcement and the media, sending letters and making phone calls, boasting about his crimes and playing mind games with investigators.

* Shawcross had a pattern of releasing his victims' bodies in or near bodies of water, including the Genesee River, which earned him the nickname "Genesee River Killer."

* He was once married and had children, but his relationships were marked by violence and abuse, and he was known to have a history of abusive behavior towards women.

* Shawcross claimed to have had sexual fantasies involving mutilation and cannibalism, and he reportedly ate parts of some of his victims' bodies.

* He had a fascination with death and often visited cemeteries, where he would perform bizarre rituals and mutilate gravesites.

* Shawcross was known to have lied and manipulated those around him, including family members, friends, and acquaintances, in order to cover up his crimes.

* He had a history of mental health issues, including a diagnosis of antisocial personality disorder, which is characterized by a lack of empathy and disregard for the rights of others.

* Shawcross was considered a high-functioning psychopath, able to blend into society and appear normal to those around him, despite his dark tendencies.

* He once claimed to have had a personal relationship with the devil, whom he referred to as "Herbert," and claimed that Herbert had instructed him to commit murder.

* Shawcross had a fascination with the occult and claimed to have practiced satanic rituals, which he believed gave him power and protection.

* He had a habit of returning to the scenes of his crimes to relive the experience, reveling in the terror and suffering he had caused.

* Shawcross had a history of failed attempts at rehabilitation and was known to have lied during psychological evaluations, downplaying his violent tendencies and minimizing his actions.

* He once attempted to escape from prison by faking a suicide attempt, but was unsuccessful.

* He made disturbing and sexually explicit drawings while in prison, depicting violent acts and mutilation.

* He stalked his victims for prolonged periods of time, meticulously planning his attacks and selecting vulnerable targets.

* Shawcross had a history of failed attempts at rehabilitation and was considered a danger to society, with mental health professionals identifying him as a high-risk individual.

* He was convicted of multiple counts of murder and sentenced to life in prison without the possibility of parole.

* Despite his heinous crimes, Shawcross continued to boast about his actions and relish in his notoriety, showing a complete lack of remorse for his victims and their families.

* Shawcross died in 2008 at the age of 63 while serving his life sentence in prison, taking with him the secrets of his true motivations and the extent of his depravity to the grave.

Henry Lee Lucas
& Ottis Toole

Evil Duo

Henry Lee Lucas and Ottis Toole were two notorious serial killers who gained infamy for their gruesome crimes and shocking depravity.

Henry Lee Lucas was born on August 23, 1936, in Blacksburg, Virginia. He grew up in an abusive household, suffering physical and psychological abuse from his alcoholic father. Lucas had a history of violent behavior from a young age and was known to have committed his first murder at the age of 14. He drifted around the country and was involved in various criminal activities, including theft and assault, before embarking on a killing spree that lasted from the 1960s to the 1980s.

Ottis Toole, on the other hand, was born on March 5, 1947, in Jacksonville, Florida. He was raised in a dysfunctional family, with his mother being a prostitute and his father a violent alcoholic. Toole had a troubled childhood, exhibiting signs of pyromania and cruelty to animals. He was known to have committed his first murder at the age of 14, and his crimes escalated to include arson, theft, and acts of violence.

Both Lucas and Toole were known to have a close relationship, having met in a Jacksonville soup kitchen in the early 1970s. They became traveling companions and committed a series of heinous crimes together, including multiple cases of rape, torture, and murder. They were known for their random and senseless acts of violence, targeting men, women, and children without discrimination.

Lucas and Toole were known to have been highly manipulative and often changed their stories, providing false confessions and contradicting their own statements. Lucas, in particular, gained notoriety for his false confessions to hundreds of murders, later recanting many of them. Despite this, they were both convicted for multiple murders, with Lucas receiving the death penalty and Toole serving multiple life sentences.

Henry Lee Lucas died of natural causes in prison on March 12, 2001, at the age of 64. Ottis Toole died in prison on September 15, 1996, at the age of 49. Their legacy as two of the most brutal and twisted serial killers in history continues to haunt those who remember their chilling reign of terror.

FACT FILE:

❖ Henry Lee Lucas and Ottis Toole were known as the "Deadly Duo" and were believed to have committed a string of murders across the United States during the 1970s and 1980s.

❖ Lucas and Toole met in a soup kitchen in Jacksonville, Florida, in the early 1970s and formed a bond that led them to embark on a murderous spree together.

❖ They were known for their random and senseless acts of violence, often targeting vulnerable individuals, including hitchhikers, prostitutes, and children.

❖ Lucas claimed to have committed over 600 murders, although this number is widely believed to be exaggerated, as he was known for providing false confessions.

❖ Toole had a history of pyromania and was known to have set fires as a form of sadistic pleasure.

❖ Both Lucas and Toole were known to have engaged in acts of cannibalism, necrophilia, and mutilation of their victims' bodies.

❖ They would often pick up hitchhikers or offer them rides, only to later torture, rape, and murder them.

* Lucas and Toole were known to have used various methods of killing, including stabbing, strangulation, and bludgeoning.

* They targeted victims of all ages, including men, women, and children, showing a complete disregard for human life.

* Lucas and Toole would often keep trophies from their victims, such as personal belongings or body parts, as mementos of their gruesome acts.

* They had a penchant for leaving behind disturbing scenes at the crime scenes, including dismembered bodies and sexually explicit displays.

* Lucas and Toole were known to have traveled extensively across the United States, committing murders in multiple states, making it difficult for law enforcement to track their movements.

* They often took pleasure in taunting law enforcement and playing cat-and-mouse games with the authorities, leaving behind cryptic messages and clues at the crime scenes.

* Lucas and Toole were known to have targeted individuals from marginalized communities, such as sex workers and members of the LGBTQ+ community, who they believed would be less likely to be missed or investigated.

* They were known to have committed acts of violence against animals, including mutilating and killing them, showing early signs of their violent tendencies.

* Lucas and Toole had a history of prior criminal offenses, including burglary, theft, and assault, before their murderous spree.

* They had a pattern of preying on vulnerable individuals, gaining their trust before turning on them and inflicting extreme violence.

* Lucas and Toole were known to have lured victims to secluded areas or abandoned buildings, where they would carry out their sadistic acts.

* They were known to have used different aliases and changed their appearances to evade capture, making it difficult for law enforcement to track them down.

* Lucas and Toole had a disturbing fascination with fire and would often set fires at crime scenes or to cover up their tracks.

* They often engaged in sexual violence, including rape and torture, as part of their sadistic acts.

* Lucas and Toole were known to have committed acts of violence against each other, showcasing their volatile and dangerous personalities.

* They were both convicted of multiple counts of murder and received lengthy prison sentences, with Lucas being sentenced to death and Toole serving multiple life sentences.

* Lucas had a troubled childhood, growing up in an abusive household with a violent father, which is believed to have contributed to his later criminal behavior.

* Toole had a history of mental illness, including schizophrenia and borderline personality disorder, which may have influenced his violent tendencies.

* Lucas and Toole would often recount their gruesome acts in detail, showing a disturbing lack of empathy or remorse for the pain and suffering they inflicted upon their victims.

* They were known to have engaged in rituals and bizarre behavior during their murders, such as mutilating bodies, consuming human flesh, and engaging in sexual acts with corpses.

* Lucas and Toole had a history of substance abuse, including heavy alcohol and drug use, which may have further fueled their violent and impulsive behavior.

Paul Bernardo
& Karla Homolka
The Ken and Barbie Killers

Paul
Bernardo and Karla Homolka are infamous figures in
Canadian criminal history, known for their gruesome and
chilling crimes. Paul Bernardo was born on August 27, 1964,
in Scarborough, Ontario, Canada. Karla Homolka was born
on May 4, 1970, in Port Credit, Ontario, Canada.

Paul Bernardo grew up in a seemingly normal middle-class
family, but early signs of disturbing behavior emerged. He
was known for his cruel treatment of animals and his
obsession with sexual violence. Bernardo's dark inclinations
continued into adulthood, and he soon became infatuated
with Karla Homolka, a young woman he met in the late
1980s.

Karla Homolka was known for her beauty and charm, but she had her own dark secrets. She was captivated by Bernardo's dark and violent fantasies, and the two embarked on a twisted and depraved relationship. Together, they committed a series of heinous crimes that sent shockwaves through the nation.

In the early 1990s, Bernardo and Homolka kidnapped, raped, and murdered three teenage girls, including Homolka's younger sister, Tammy. The brutality of their crimes was chilling, involving sadistic sexual torture and murder. They filmed some of their horrific acts, creating evidence that would later come back to haunt them.

The duo's reign of terror came to an end in 1993 when they were arrested by authorities. Their trial was a media spectacle, and the details of their crimes were revealed in all their gruesome horror. Bernardo was eventually convicted of multiple counts of first-degree murder, aggravated sexual assault, and kidnapping, and he received a life sentence without the possibility of parole for 25 years. Homolka, on the other hand, struck a plea deal with prosecutors, which led to her serving only 12 years in prison for manslaughter.

Despite their vile crimes, Bernardo and Homolka remain notorious figures in Canadian criminal history. Their chilling biography serves as a haunting reminder of the depths of human depravity and the horrors that can be committed by those who walk among us.

FACT FILE:

❖ Paul Bernardo, also known as the "Scarborough Rapist," and Karla Homolka, his wife, were a notorious Canadian couple who committed a series of heinous crimes in the 1990s.

❖ Paul Bernardo was born on August 27, 1964, in Scarborough, Ontario, Canada, while Karla Homolka was born on May 4, 1970, in Port Credit, Ontario, Canada.

❖ Paul Bernardo had a history of cruelty towards animals from a young age, often torturing and killing them, which was considered an early warning sign of his violent tendencies.

❖ Karla Homolka was known for her striking beauty and was described as charming and outgoing, which made her an unsuspecting accomplice in the crimes committed by Bernardo.

❖ Paul Bernardo and Karla Homolka met in the late 1980s and became romantically involved, quickly escalating into a toxic relationship based on their shared dark fantasies.

❖ They kidnapped, raped, and murdered three teenage girls, including Karla Homolka's younger sister, Tammy, whom they drugged and sexually assaulted before she died.

* The couple filmed their horrific acts, creating video tapes that would later be discovered by police and used as evidence against them during their trial.

* Paul Bernardo and Karla Homolka were known for their sadistic sexual torture, which included inflicting extreme pain and suffering on their victims.

* They would often dress up their victims in revealing outfits and engage in depraved sexual acts before killing them.

* Paul Bernardo and Karla Homolka's crimes were known for their extreme brutality, involving prolonged torture, mutilation, and murder.

* They often used a combination of drugs and alcohol to incapacitate their victims, making them helpless and easier to control.

* Paul Bernardo and Karla Homolka displayed a disturbing level of premeditation and planning in their crimes, carefully selecting their victims and executing their sadistic fantasies.

* They had a "kill kit," which included various tools and supplies used to commit their crimes, hidden in their home.

* Paul Bernardo and Karla Homolka's crimes terrorized the community, with fear spreading rapidly as they continued to evade capture.

* They taunted law enforcement and the media, sending anonymous letters and making phone calls to revel in the attention their crimes received.

* Despite the horrific nature of their crimes, Paul Bernardo and Karla Homolka maintained a facade of normalcy in their everyday lives, presenting themselves as a typical couple to those around them.

* Karla Homolka portrayed herself as a victim of abuse at the hands of Paul Bernardo during their trial, claiming that she was coerced into participating in the crimes.

* However, evidence later revealed that Karla Homolka was a willing and active participant in the crimes, and she had actively assisted Bernardo in carrying out his sadistic desires.

* Paul Bernardo was eventually caught in 1993 when he was caught attempting to abduct another young woman, leading to his arrest and the discovery of the evidence against him.

* During their trial, the details of Paul Bernardo and Karla Homolka's crimes shocked the nation.

* In 1995, Paul Bernardo was convicted of multiple counts of firs-degree murder, aggravated sexual assault, and kidnapping, and he received a life sentence without the possibility of parole for 25 years.

* Karla Homolka struck a plea deal with prosecutors, pleading guilty to manslaughter in exchange for a reduced sentence of 12 years in prison, which sparked outrage and controversy among the public and the victims' families.

* After serving her 12-year sentence, Karla Homolka was released from prison in 2005 and changed her name, assuming a new identity to start a new life.

* Paul Bernardo, on the other hand, remains in prison to this day, considered one of Canada's most notorious and dangerous criminals.

* In 2018, it was revealed that Karla Homolka had been volunteering at her children's elementary school, which sparked further public outrage and concern for the safety of the children.

* The video tapes created by Paul Bernardo and Karla Homolka, documenting their sadistic acts, are considered some of the most disturbing and horrifying pieces of evidence in criminal history.

Afterword

The world of serial killers is a chilling and terrifying place. These individuals have left a legacy of violence and fear, and their actions have caused immense suffering and trauma to countless innocent victims and their families.

The study of serial killers may be fascinating to some, but it is important to remember that these individuals are highly dangerous and unpredictable. They often display a pattern of violent behavior, with an insatiable desire to harm and kill others. These killers often blend in with society, and can be your neighbor, your co-worker, or even your friend.

Their ability to hide in plain sight is what makes them so terrifying. It is difficult to know who among us may be capable of such heinous acts. However, there are often warning signs that can indicate potential violent behavior, such as a history of abuse or neglect, a fascination with death or violence, and a lack of empathy or remorse.

The consequences of ignoring these warning signs can be devastating. Lives can be lost, families can be destroyed, and communities can be left in fear. The aftermath of a serial killer's actions can leave a lasting impact on the lives of those affected.

We must work together as a society to prevent future tragedies by educating ourselves on the warning signs of potential violent behavior and intervening early to stop these individuals before they are able to cause harm. This includes taking action when we see something concerning, such as reporting suspicious behavior to authorities.

We must also prioritize the safety and wellbeing of our communities by investing in mental health resources, victim support services, and law enforcement training. These efforts can help to prevent future tragedies and ensure that our society remains a safe and peaceful place for all.

In the end, the legacy of serial killers should serve as a chilling reminder of the evil that exists in the world, and the importance of remaining vigilant and aware of the warning signs of potential violent behavior. By working together, we can prevent future tragedies and build a better and safer society for all.

— *J. Sutton Parkside*

*If you found The Ultimate Serial Killer Fact File
informative and thought-provoking, I would greatly
appreciate it if you could take a moment to leave a review
on Amazon. Your feedback is invaluable and helps other
readers discover the book. Thank you for your support!*

— J. S. P.

Printed in Great Britain
by Amazon

22671444R00145